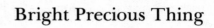

Bright Precious Thing

Bright
Precious
Thing

A Memoir

Gail Caldwell

RANDOM HOUSE
NEW YORK

Published in the United States by Random House,
an imprint and division of Penguin Random House LLC, New York.

RANDOM HOUSE and the HOUSE colophon are
registered trademarks of Penguin Random House LLC.

LIBRARY OF CONGRESS CATALOGING-IN-PUBLICATION DATA
Names: Caldwell, Gail, author.
Title: Bright precious thing: a memoir / Gail Caldwell.
Description: New York: Random House, 2020.
Identifiers: LCCN 2019026880 (print) | LCCN 2019026881 (ebook)
| ISBN 9780525510055 (hardcover) | ISBN 9780525510062 (ebook)
Subjects: LCSH: Caldwell, Gail | Journalists—United States—
Biography. | Critics—United States—Biography.
Classification: LCC PN4874.C2187 A3 2020 (print) |
LCC PN4874.C2187 (ebook) | DDC 070.92 [B]—dc23
LC record available at https://lccn.loc.gov/2019026880
LC ebook record available at https://lccn.loc.gov/2019026881

Printed in the United States of America on acid-free paper

randomhousebooks.com

1 2 3 4 5 6 7 8 9

First Edition

Book design by Susan Turner

For Louise Erdrich
and for Jaylin and Rafi

The great revelation perhaps never did come. Instead there were little daily miracles, illuminations, matches struck unexpectedly in the dark; here was one.

Virginia Woolf, *To the Lighthouse*

Bright Precious Thing

Cambridge, 2015

My Samoyed is looking out the glass storm door to the street when I see her ears go back with pleasure. Tyler walks in and crouches down to nuzzle the dog, who outweighs her by about fifteen pounds, and then announces herself with the usual certainty, as though she's on a tight schedule and has been gone only a few minutes. "We had early release," she tells me, "so I was able to get here on time." Tyler is five, and lives two doors away, and passes my house on her way to the neighborhood park. She has the countenance of a small superhero. When she was three she became enamored with Tula, a fluffy white creature who shares her affection, and now we are an essential stop on the trail of Tyler's day. I make it a point to stock up on the dark chocolate wafers she likes. When she leaves town for a week on family vacation, my house feels as quiet as a cinder block. Then the door flies open one morning and I hear her shout: "I'm back!"

Today we're lying on the back porch and planning what to do if we are marooned on a desert island—what we will choose to take. We can each have three items. Tyler decides that she will take a rope, a boat (which is broken, or why would she be there?), and a knife. For food she will take two Popsicles, an ice cream bar, and Jell-O.

Ignoring the fact that she has doubled her allotment, I suggest that she toss in a roast chicken and some milk. She agrees, knowing the milk, as she tells me, will make her strong until her mother arrives. Her rope will be blue, will be 250,000-plus-infinity miles long. That way, if her mother is late, the rope can be thrown wide, and reach land on the other side of the ocean.

I marvel that she has any idea what infinity is, though this is a mutual learning society: She reminds me of the innocence of forward motion, and I try to give her a palette for all that hope. I tell her a story about a surfer girl, lost at sea, who was hungry and alone. Then she remembered her mother's teaching her the constellations as a means of navigation. If she held up her fingers to the sky, she could use the celestial map to fix her position in space, and chart her way back to land.

"Everything you need to know is in the sky," I tell Tyler, and we look up through our fingers, content in that zone of serenity that children can elicit. I don't tell her that I learned the story about the surfer girl from *Hawaii Five-0*, or that the girl's mother was long dead, and that the girl was actually a woman cop who was hallucinating and dehydrated and nearly died at sea. Tyler will get to tragedy soon enough. For now the lost girls can have all the ice cream they want, and mothers who are on their way, and their journeys only have to be as far as a couple of houses down.

Around the time Tyler first appeared at my door, I was starting a book about growing up female in Texas, and about the profound influence that feminism—the women's movement of the 1970s—had on my life. I came of age in the Panhandle, a stronghold of Protestant churches and Republican politics where the sky goes on forever. I left for college in 1968: The year that Martin Luther King, Jr., and Bobby Kennedy were shot and Nixon was elected. The year of My Lai and the Tet Offensive. Student protestors at Columbia shut the place down; women stormed the stage at the Miss America pageant. It was one of the most tumultuous and exalted times in modern history, and I was seventeen and felt like I'd been shot out of a cannon. Within a few years I went from being a bookish girl with a head for numbers to an anti-war protestor and young feminist with a wet bandanna in my back pocket, to shield my face from tear gas.

That's some expedition for a kid who spent her days reading at the town library and playing jacks with her sister. And it's light-years from the world of the brown girl daydreaming on my porch in Cambridge a half century later—who by age five was quoting lines and singing lyrics from *Hamilton*. "Are you an immigrant?" Tyler asked me one day, conflating Texas with some place weird and far away. And then, in the words of Lin-Manuel Miranda, "Because immigrants, we get the job done."

I realized pretty quickly that this story belonged to us both.

Part of what sent me back to my salad days was a quest to set the record straight. In the decades since I wandered into my first women's liberation rally on the University of Texas campus, in the early 1970s, "feminism" had morphed into a dirty word in the lexicon. "I'm not a feminist, but . . ." The phrase baffled and irritated me. Oversimplified and sometimes demonized, the idea of feminism—at least the old-school, second-wave version—had come to suggest liberal white privilege, where the victories had been in the boardroom instead of the streets. And young women who were realizing triumphs of the movement were now in danger of disparaging or forgetting it altogether.

That an alliance with feminism came with a qualifier was a shock to me. The feminism that I knew was not bourgeois, exclusive, or, God forbid, boring. It was radical and often joyful and it quite possibly saved my life. The seismic encounters of adolescence had changed me from a levelheaded introvert to a wild girl and a cliff diver, ill-equipped to withstand the onslaught of sex, drugs, and rock and roll that defined my generation. The traditional paths of marriage and motherhood seemed lethal in a whole other way. The women's movement delivered me from both fates. It offered a scaffolding of sanity and self-respect, a way to get a grip on everything that was scary about life. And in those days, when the blueprint for adulthood was being questioned daily or even set on fire, life could be scary indeed.

I started writing a reflection of that time, a personal story that began with a half-lost, frightened college girl on her way to class in Texas. In two different cities I read aloud a portion of the chapter, and during the first reading I was startled to see young women in the audience in tears. Maybe I had touched a known pain. Later that year at a teaching weekend, I talked to and read the work of women who were under thirty, many of whom knew a whole different kind of trouble, and I recognized something else in their voices—raw but also angry and determined. This time when I read the piece, the reaction was not tears but nods and half-raised fists. So I went home and kept writing. They had touched something in me, too.

Pastiches began to emerge of incidents I hadn't thought about in years: hurdles cleared or dodged, egregious insults I'd put behind me. I knew I was remembering a story mystifying or foreign to men but next-door familiar to women, whether they grew up in Texas or Greenwich Village, in high cotton or hard times. All of us had been trained to take less than her share at the table, and some of us even hated and feared each other because that's what pressure from above teaches and forces an underclass to do.

I wanted to take back the words and memories, just like we took back the night several decades ago, when I wore my TBTN T-shirt until it hung from me in shreds. The Take Back the Night movement was the start of mass demonstrations against sexual and domestic violence, and people marched in Austin and Atlanta and

New York in the 1970s, thousands of us, to gain access to time and light as well as space: Give me back what should already be mine. Give me the dark, the freedom of the streets, the right to walk wherever I want, unafraid of rape or assault or just being messed with. The stars belong to me as much as you. Move over. Make room on the bench.

The lessons of those days were so basic: To view other women as allies rather than the competition. To unleash our intelligence, liberate our bodies, assume we were capable of things previously denied or unconsidered. We could be mathematicians, car mechanics, soccer players instead of cheerleaders. If this sounds obvious today, it's because we took over buildings and challenged male professors who told us we didn't have the brains for science or that we were cute when we were mad. The fight felt vital and dangerous, and often it was both. And when I feel hopeless or alone, or when all that seems a long time ago, I have to remind myself that—no other way to say it—a lot of what we did and said really did change the world.

We were heady with how much we knew, which was sometimes less than what we built our mettle on. But it was uplifting and even thrilling to realize you could replace a fan belt or build a bookshelf, even if you did it badly or it took four hours. We started all-girl rock and roll bands and law collectives; we played drums on the beach and argued about class struggle and grew our own food. We all thought, for a while, that we had broken free.

The struggle was hard-won, especially when the worst demons in the room were mine. The feminist notions so easily embraced as theory—that women internalize anger as depression; that power often eludes us in the service of being good—are brutally difficult to change. So this is partly a story about the soldering of self: about the paths and stumbles I took, into shadow and out again. But all that exposure to women's autonomy had given me muscle I didn't know I had. Long before I'd read a word of Virginia Woolf, I knew that, for me, a room of one's own was the ultimate prize. That a lock on the door was the power to think for oneself.

As stories go, mine is pretty tame. There are countless far worse ones, where women in heinous situations of violence and predation had no way out. And there are several orders of magnitude between, say, a jerk on the street and one holding the deed to your house, or strafing your neighborhood in Aleppo. I recognize this and try to remember it, every day.

I had the resources to jump free of circumstance, among them a father who loved me and a mother whose own untended dreams fostered mine. I also had a library—Joan of Arc; Jody and the fawn; Cherry Ames, war nurse. Tomboys and androgynes and adventure girls, *c'est moi,* and they shaped me long before I got to my preferred tragic heroines, to the likes of Emma Bovary or Tess of the D'Urbervilles. And later: Joan Didion, Lillian Hellman, Mary McCarthy.

I read these women when I was on the brink of adulthood, avoiding the window of the future because everything good seemed either frightening or impossible. But there was something irresistible about the brashness, the insolence, of becoming a writer, and its draw was even bigger than my fear. I had dropped out of college and wandered around California and come back to Austin, and I'd worked as a paralegal and a vegetarian restaurant hash slinger, when the culture allowed one to spend years as a ne'er-do-well. Now I was mostly sleeping late and swimming laps at Barton Springs and drinking in Texas bars. On the sly I read the critics for *The Village Voice* and *The New York Review of Books,* particularly the mouthy women, and I thought, secretly, *I could do that.*

"Silence, exile, and cunning." Those were James Joyce's weapons of choice, words he gave to Stephen Dedalus in *A Portrait of the Artist as a Young Man.* I have an old edition of the novel from 1966, when I would have been fifteen. Its binding is broken from age and use, and that quote—penciled in my teenage cursive, "silence exile cunning"—is written hurriedly, without commas, on both end pages of the book, as though I might need the words as a prompt to get out fast. And I've translated the Latin epigraph *Et ignotas animum dimittit in artes,* from Ovid's *Metamorphoses.* Again, my loopy, innocent-looking script: "And he set his mind to unknown arts."

It may as well have been "unknown parts," given how vast I imagined my odyssey. That Joyce's artist was a young man either made no impression or didn't hold me back at all. So maybe that was my religious text, me and a million other pilgrims, all of us clutching Hesse or Joyce or Kerouac and trying our wings. My primer of the writer as a young Texas female, headed north toward home.

Plan a book and the muses laugh. All this came before the 2016 presidential race. When Donald Trump announced his candidacy the previous summer, I whooped at the absurdity and bet a friend $10 he wouldn't last ten days.

In the next two years the everyday trials of being female went from a background burn to a cacophony of outrage and catharsis. I need to believe that moral courage will win out over iniquity, but a whole lot of horrible has already happened, and the devastation of the Trump years is not yet finished. Still, the anger and momentum of the past few years have given me hope, too. That we haven't forgotten the lessons of history, and that we remembered how to fight.

Something else had a hold of me during this time, as meaningful and as loaded with power as the headlines were frightening. A small, shy girl, new to the neighborhood, knocked on my door one day, her mother beside her, because she had seen my dog and wanted to meet her. The mother was gracious and apologetic, the child unforgettable. Tula rolled over and wagged her tail and the deal was done. Tyler had free access to my house and to me from then on, and so began a two-way avenue of peach cobblers and water fights and perfect summer afternoons. She has probably taught me far more than I have her.

Everything we need is in the sky, I told Tyler that day on the porch. Is this true? Airplanes, imagined deities kind and angry, light, water, color, hope. Also: bombers, drones, acid rain, things falling. The ancients believed a solar eclipse was the end of the world. My friends and

I watch a lunar eclipse in autumn, and while people pass around mugs of cider and rum I get a crick in my neck from staring at the moon—its lessening sphere that turns orange-red before it disappears. I can't take my eyes off it, afraid I will miss something critical, some sign before its end. Is that a high-drama metaphor, the world turning itself into an angry red as it waves good-bye? We so take the sky for granted. Its staggering blue color, cloying anywhere else, impossible to imitate. Ever since 9/11 it hints at tragedy. Throw every other form against it—bridges, say, or dirigibles, or oil rigs—and you still have that background explosion of light announcing itself each dawn. Saying, *I was here first; just try doing anything funny without going through me.*

Now we've screwed it all up, but I didn't tell Tyler that, either. Any five-year-old who can count to 250,000-plus-infinity has the imagination to save the sky and the courage to die trying.

So: This book is for the women. This is for Inez Garcia, who was raped in 1974—who went home and got a .22 rifle and shot one of her attackers dead. She was convicted of second-degree murder and served two years in state prison before the verdict was overturned. It's for Recy Taylor, a sharecropper whose gang rape was investigated by a woman named Rosa Parks, years before Parks refused to give up her seat on that bus. This is for Debbie Sharpe, a Texas friend who died at the hands of her stalker. It's for the dead-poet sister Virginia Woolf imagined for Shakespeare, for Sister Carrie, for the sluts and wallflowers and junkies who didn't get as far as the door that Ibsen's Nora slammed. It's for two of my aunts who were blasted with electro-shock therapy, because there was no other treatment then for women who were depressed or alcoholic or just downright sick of it all.

And it's for the boys, too. The good sons who are learning how to be good men. It's for everyone ahead of us, the people inheriting this place, this war-torn ground.

2

It was my good fortune to have a father who was blustery and kind and adored his daughters, and whose worst faults—anger and stubbornness—were sometimes put to use in protection of us.

My dad was a master sergeant in the Second World War, stationed for three years near Blackpool, England, where he was in charge of operations on a supply base for the European theater. On payday, the men in his company were granted leave to go roam the pubs in town. M.Sgt. Caldwell, who loved a drink as much as anyone, usually stayed behind on base. After his men came back to meet the midnight curfew, many of them having stayed too long at the bar, he'd ask if anyone wanted to play cards. He was a farm boy from Texas, and he had a sweet, low way of talking that throughout his life made him seem trustworthy, which in turn made him a dangerously good poker player.

He came home from England in 1946 with a money belt hidden on his waist. That was how he put a down payment on the little house in Amarillo, Texas, that he and my mom bought after the war: from the winnings he made on Friday nights. He taught me to play cards when I was four.

An element of that family legend became more resonant to me after my father's death. The ninth of ten children, he was raised on a struggling farm in east Texas, and his family worked so hard to put food on the table that he remembered his finest Christmas as the one when every child got an orange. His eyes shone when he told us about that orange. And though I spent most of my childhood thinking he was a fearless and invincible man, I know now that the one thing that terrified him was poverty.

The poker story changes when you realize that the master sergeant was a barefoot boy from Sulphur Springs, trying to wile his way out of the lion's mouth. He picked cotton in the fields when he was little, and he told me that two of his older sisters, one on either side of him in the Texas sun, had taught him how to count to ten by using his knuckles. Then he got a little older, and his five brothers showed him how to use his knuckles in another way. Even after he put himself through college by working three jobs, he declared those two early lessons the most valuable of his life.

We fought for decades about politics, and often it was senseless and ugly, and we could bring out the worst in each other. I was prideful and high-minded; he called me stupid and said I knew nothing about the world. He was an old-fashioned conservative Democrat who went over to Nixon and Reagan; I went home from Austin wearing jeans with a Vietcong flag embroidered on my ass, thrilled at my ability to infuriate him. What fools we were. He always contended that half of life was knowing how to bluff, and fifteen years after his death, I no longer think that's just funny but also, regrettably, true.

My sister texted me during the weeks before the election and wrote, *How would Dad have voted? A real dilemma.*

I wrote back, fast: *No dilemma. Hillary.*

Her answer, surprised and skeptical and no doubt trying to avoid a tirade from me: *Why? What would he have thought of Trump? One word.*

Me: *Two words. Six bankruptcies.*

Then again: *Two more: Sexual bully.*

Her response. *Really laughing out loud. In fact guffawing.* We may have been remembering the same thing.

. . .

The hundred acres in east Texas where my dad had grown up was swamp-and-mosquito land, planted with cotton and watermelon. His parents, Pink and Della, had both died before I was born, and the house they built, with ten-foot ceilings and no indoor plumbing, was where we all gathered for family reunions. By the 1950s, when I was born, it was mostly a place of memories and card games and tall tales. There was the long table where Della had fed her ten kids, where my dad remembered eating as fast as he could before she ran out of second helpings. There was the bedroom he'd shared with his brothers, the setting for one of his scariest stories: When he was eight, he told us, he got up in the night to go use the outhouse, and noted, half-asleep, that his pillow seemed lumpy. He came back to bed and turned the pillow over, and in the moonlit dark saw a poisonous copperhead, coiled where his head had been. He hated snakes from then on, and I, his prankster daughter, loved to sneak up behind him with colored photos from the reptile section of the encyclopedia. He always bellowed in mock terror, or so I assumed. It was unthinkable to me that he might actually be afraid of a little snake.

"The farm," we called it, even though my maternal

grandparents also lived on a farm closer to us and visited more often. But Della and Pink's place would forever be *the* farm, singular fount of my father's stories, and stays so in my mind's eye. Of all the aunts and uncles and cousins, our family had to drive the farthest: clear across Texas, from Amarillo to Sulphur Springs, which took us about ten hours. There was always a crush of cousins, with my sister and me—she was two years older—on the quiet fringe of the crowd. We were both readers, for which we were teased, and though she was a tomboy, she usually held back long enough to keep an eye on me.

The latch on the outhouse door had been broken for as long as I knew. I can still smell the earthen lime we used as a scoop, see the shadowy sunlight between the slats. The outhouse may have been an icon of rural poverty, but it was not a scary place. Kids are practical and rarely squeamish. When we were playing tag or war in the field beyond the house, the shed offered quick, efficient relief.

But as with that snake in my dad's sleeping quarters, the outhouse had an unwelcome visitor. Lance was a few years older than us, and the leader of the boy cousins. Most of us tried to avoid him or followed meekly in his path; those were the obvious options. His torments were mercurial—like most bullies, he bored easily—and one summer when he was twelve or thirteen he turned his sights on the girls.

We usually guarded each other at the outhouse because of the broken latch. Lance's strategy was to lie in wait until one of us had to go, then shove the spotter out of the way and fling open the outhouse door. Most outhouses are simple sheds surrounding a wooden platform with a hole built over a deep trench. Whoever is inside is fully exposed if the door is open.

My sister was older and bigger and she stood up to Lance, and he never got past her to humiliate me. But I remember a year when the girls spent their days in fear of Lance's attention, being too afraid to pee or waiting for the brief window when he wasn't watching.

I don't remember who told. Probably one of the younger cousins, for whom silence was not yet a code of honor. And I never knew which adult they approached, only that my dad was the one who would intervene. He waited until the next day when all the kids were playing in the field, and he strolled over to Lance with a smile on his face. Then he picked him up in an overhead hold and held him there, the way a rancher might hold a thrashing calf. My dad had been a middleweight wrestler in college, and the move was probably easy for him. He talked to his dangling nephew in a whisper-quiet voice, and then he put him down, almost gently. Lance was very still. None of us kids could hear what was said. But Lance never bothered us again.

All the uncles took Lance on a snipe hunt that night—a classic prank in east Texas that sent a boy into the woods for a few hours in search of an imagined prey. But I suspect the die was already cast by my father's swift maneuver in the field. The bully had been out-bullied by someone twice his size and age, in the name of protecting his daughters.

I idealized my father, both before and since his death, and that tough, low voice that terrorized Lance that day was one I knew well. But I was never scared of him, because I was part of the castle that the dragon was defending. Good news for me, less so for cousin Lance.

More than half a century later, I think my father's selective force was more an asset to me than a burden. With his sometimes infuriating Texas swagger, he provided a world of jokes and monsters—outhouses and snakes and blackguard cousins—and then proved it was manageable by swooping in at the right moment. His confidence and his love took; they made me brave, later on, when I needed to be. Invaluable lessons for a girl in the Texas Panhandle on the cusp of the 1960s: that somebody had my back, and that I was somebody worth saving.

TYLER'S T-SHIRT LEGEND SAYS GIRL POWER, WITH several descriptors on its front: SMART, ARTIST, STRONG. I try to turn the T-shirt into a reading lesson but she bores quickly: She's already memorized all the words, and seems to assume she is or will be all those things. Instead she wants to run hurdles in the back-yard, and has the idea of building an agility course for Tula. Soon I am setting up brooms and rakes slung across lawn chairs, low jumps that become increasingly challenging. Then I am holding my breath while the girl and the dog, my precious charges, make their way through a maze of obstacles without a hitch. And then I am hollering encouragement, timing Tyler's laps on my phone's stopwatch. A small Usain Bolt is flying through and over our makeshift track. *"How fast?"* she calls after the last jump, after I have yelled *"Go go go you've got it!"* Finally we all collapse on the cool grass. Tyler is pleased and spent; Tula is panting; I'm hoarse from cheering, a cross between a soccer mom and Bill Belichick. Now I understand how parents find them-selves in bouncy castles.

"You are raising me really badly," I say later. We are dipping strawberries in the sugar bowl, something she convinced me to try after I'd admonished her for doing it. The rules over here are pretty lax. But when Tyler starts to fantasize about what an actual sleepover would be like, I up the ante. Military drills, I say. A bugle call, then jumping jacks, at five A.M. Cold cereal for breakfast, but only after you clean the basement. *"And then what?"* she cries. She adores this story. Every story we make up delights us both.

3

Weeks before the 2016 election, I was in the South End in Boston, having dinner with a friend, when the audio-video broke of Trump bragging about his sexual prowess to Billy Bush. Sick of the ever-present news cycle, I had gone off the grid for a few hours, and when I hit my phone at ten P.M., I was deluged with texts: "Did you see?" "It's all over." The next several days were an information blitz: With four weeks to go before the election, a dozen women came forward and accused the Republican nominee of sexual misconduct.

Social media maven Kelly Oxford posted something on Twitter that prompted an explosion in return. "Women: tweet me your first assaults," she wrote on the night of the Bush videotape release. "I'll go first: Old man on city bus grabs my 'pussy' and smiles at me, I'm 12."

She later told an interviewer she expected only a handful of responses. By the end of the day after her posting, she had more than a million.

For every woman I knew, the story about the tape was appalling, Oxford's responses mind-blowing, but none of it was unfamiliar. A lot of women wrote the tweet equivalent of a shrug: "Sure. Which assault? First or worst?" It became a grim parlor game. I texted a friend that I had counted to fifteen and then paused, having to reconsider my criteria. *Do I count the flashers when I'm rowing on the river?* I wrote her. *In which case it's way more than fifteen. What about the time the guy tried to grab my breast on a plane but I blocked his arm?*

Wow you have way more than me, she wrote back, remembering a clumsy sexual pass by a fellow musician whom she slugged. *That's because you married at twenty-seven,* I shot back. *Husbands protect you.* (Some of them, I should have added.) *Chattel. I'm remembering things from way back. Like the time a colleague grabbed me in an empty newsroom and stuck his tongue in my mouth. Tried to, anyway.*

Humor saved us, but it also shielded old anger, and mine called up deep, embedded messages: How to block a pass, walk faster on a dark street, cross a parking lot alone, make eye contact, yell, cajole, outtalk, run, carry your keys between your knuckles, get a whistle, learn judo. A survival guide to being female.

In the days between that first bombshell and the election itself, I felt dry-mouthed, pissed off, ready to spring. I swam harder to calm myself down, talked faster because I couldn't help it. My typical reaction to calamitous events, personal and societal, was not like this. I tend to get calm in a crisis, fall apart later, and have a pretty good ego barrier between global terrors and the monsters in my own closet. When 9/11 happened, I shared a collective shock and heartbreak, but I didn't think I was next. When the Boston Marathon bombers were being pursued in my neighborhood and we were under orders to shelter in place, I spent a lot of the day reassuring people who called, especially the friend in Texas who asked if I had a gun. Most awful things that happen in the world are not about me. It helps sometimes, not always, to know that.

The swell of memory that spread over those next few weeks couldn't be captured by front page coverage. You could see it in the eyes of women on the street, hear it in our locker rooms, wake up dreaming about it. Something toxic had been unleashed, some archive of shame and ancient past, and it was hard to look at without the old cultural strictures of defeat and fatalism. The headlock of the status quo. Fear and silence, two powerful, invisible weapons, once kept the darker elements of being female in a cloistered space, unshared and even unremembered. We still roll our eyes or sigh. Why did so many women vote for Trump? I asked an old friend in Texas. How do they rationalize at least ten public accusations of sexual assault?

"They don't care," she said, weariness in her voice. "Or they don't believe them. Or they say it's always been this way." The specious reasoning of history, where the past is used to justify an intolerable present.

The spring of 2016 had been spectacular, everything in bloom twice over, and a friend from Texas whom I'd known for thirty-five years came to visit. We walked around the narrow backstreets of Cambridge near the river, where nineteenth-century workers' cottages were converted into small palaces of order, climbing roses and peonies draped over little hand-painted signs like END THE WAR NOW (which war? who knew?) and ATTENTION: CHIEN BIZARRE. All of it so insufferably, wonderfully Cambridge.

"This is your place now, isn't it?" Shannon asked me. "The East." Maybe this meandering neighborhood walk had finally cinched it for her, some thirty years after I'd left Texas. A month later an extreme drought hit New England, and our lush fortress of green now seemed fragile and fleeting. The ennui mirrored the political climate. What had begun as verdant and promising was turning into scorched earth. In September I escaped to the South Shore, where I walked the coastline and watched the dog herd the waves. One evening when the beach was emptying, I laid my clothes on a high rock—I had left my suit in the car, a mile back—and went swimming in my underwear.

Sacred moment, that, when you go in on instinct, close your eyes, and let the waves carry you. Dive into the wave. If you get caught in a riptide don't fight it. Swim parallel to the shore, and if you get tired, float on your back. Look at the sky and remember that most of life is bigger than you and your fear. Let your body be a vessel of air atop water, your lungs filling with the life force that will be your raft. Don't thrash, as this will only make you sink, make the water your enemy. The water and the earth are never your enemies; they are not interested in you, so it is your job to work with, not against, the forces of nature. Then you can survive and even feel joy as you disappear into the wave, no rocks in your pockets, not yet; this is not the River Ouse. Your T-shirt is waiting on the rocks, on land, where the real enemies are. But first let the sea remind you about strength and grace.

Because really, it's always about sheltering in place.

. . .

I took shelter that autumn in the usual places: the swimming pool, the woods with the dog, an AA meeting I've gone to for thirty-plus years. AA: for me, an institute of higher learning for the human heart. This particular meeting hosts a far-flung demographic, like most of AA, except that it's usually about a nine-to-one attendance ratio of men to women. I feel known there, and respected, and trust most of the guys to have my back in a minute. I had no problem walking into that room the week after the election and saying I felt angry, unnerved. A lot of them did, too.

One night after a meeting I was standing in the parking lot with two good friends, men I've cared about for decades, and I was telling them how women were swapping stories about being harassed. About being messed with on the job or the street. I realized my voice had gotten a little higher, my throat tightened. And G., an easy six two and as physically self-possessed as he is funny and soft-spoken, said that everyone, male and female, had to go through certain rites of humiliation; the boot camp of being alive was gender-free and primal. I paused, thinking *No no no* and also thinking that my argument wasn't, couldn't be, neutral. And then my other friend spoke up, W., a runner with the soul of a poet. He said, "No, I don't ever remember feeling that way. Not *this* way," his switch from "that" to "this" bringing me into his circle of memory. "Not this threatened." And I said that I had been counting incidents—call them macro-aggressions—and had stopped counting around twenty, which on the timeline was only about halfway through my long life.

What a Molotov cocktail that turned out to be. I was half-laughing when I said it, because I presumed we all knew. I thought everybody knew. And yet the shock on their faces—I'd unwittingly brought them in on a conversation that women have been having all their lives. W. said something so unexpected and somber that it brought tears to my eyes, brought me out of my tough-hombre narrator role. "I am so, so sorry that happened to you," he said. "My God. I had no idea."

Words had been tumbling out of me, talking to these men I loved, and everything I was saying was true, even if it was couched in my own bravado or humor to make it bearable. I wanted to break the code of silence between men and women. "Why do you think I walk around with a fifty-pound dog?" I said. "It levels the playing field."

A few days later I am outside my house picking up the newspapers when a man who lives a few streets over comes at me to say hello. For years he has assumed this approach. He's twice my size, friendly but overbearing, and his idea of hello is an uninvited bone-crushing hug. And usually I smile and wince, try to fend him off. But today is different. Today I have already heard of a group of young boys grabbing a girl in the schoolyard, saying, "Trump is going to be our president, so we can do this now." Today I am livid, sick of carrying around a lifetime of forgiveness for strangers and oafs. So when he approaches, his arms outreached, I pivot and face him, my arm up to block the pass, and something in my eyes stops him cold. He is like the Road Runner braking before the cliff; he fumbles, then thrusts out a hand instead. I shake it, hard, while his other arm flails in space. He sputters. "Would you like a hug?"

I smile and say, "No, I'm good, thanks," and this does the job. He looks deflated, like a dog who understands a growl. When I turn to walk down my driveway I feel a rush of endorphins. So this is how it feels to make them go away, instead of apologizing for their idiocy, for boys being boys. Instead of internalizing all that rage, turning it into shame or despair. Using the sword instead of swallowing it.

4

I emerged into the world beyond Amarillo a shy, lanky girl with one serious heartbreak behind me and a semi-secret desire to study mathematics. In the ninth grade I'd been blessed with a severe and passionate algebra teacher, Mrs. Springer, who had lost a breast to cancer and chose not to mask it. She was tall, thin, serious, and wore formfitting sweaters that emphasized her angular asymmetry.

There was something breathtaking about Mrs. Springer's brazenness. It was as though she had seen the worst, and still gone on to hammer the binomial theorem into her students. She seemed fearless, and those of us who weren't afraid of her would do anything to please her.

I don't know when or if I ever linked Mrs. Springer's

one-breasted warrior status to the myth about the Amazons, that they cut off a breast because it got in the way of their bow. I do know that my redheaded teacher was critical to my self-regard as well as education: she with her holy chalk and her to-hell-with-it, half-flattened chest. I was thirteen, and I worshipped her. She recognized in me some aptitude and yearning for math that made her tender toward me. One day she pulled me aside from the mean-girl cheerleaders I desperately wanted to impress.

The advice that she gave me—that a brain for math was more important than cheerleading or popularity—I could only partly absorb. I was on the verge of adolescence, when I would go from no breasts to all breasts at alarming speed, and when the beauty of mathematics was a private sanctuary for me, not something for which I wanted to sacrifice friends or boys. I didn't yet realize there would be a choice. Why would being smart have anything to do with being in love? Couldn't you swoon over polynomials and the Beatles at the same time?

Mrs. Springer's nudging and my standardized math scores carried me a certain distance, far enough for me to declare mathematics as a major when I got to college in 1968. My first two years of college were at Texas Tech University in Lubbock, a serious cattle town two hours south of Amarillo, and I spent most of my first semester trying to survive an honors calculus course that met five days a week. I was one of four girls in a class of about fifty. We scattered ourselves wide across the room from the first day, as though we were afraid to be seen in one another's company. Our chunky, gravel-voiced teacher chain-smoked—four packs of Kents a day, he announced—and covered the chalkboard in elegant, incomprehensible loops and curves. He tensed his buttocks muscles continuously as he stood at the board. This made him a foil for half the class.

I probably remember his physical tic because of how heartless Professor Mean turned out to be. I could not grasp what he was teaching. All of my quicksilver learning skills in algebra and trigonometry were gone. I studied for hours for the midterm—the first time in my life I'd ever had to study math—and still came in dismally. The professor scorned the females—three of us had done poorly, and half the class had flunked the exam. He had a private meeting with each of the girls, where we were counseled, with brutal nonchalance, to drop the class. Girls didn't belong in calculus, he told me, and my grade proved it. By December, only one woman was left; I had already fled, with shame and relief.

Well, so what? I won't entirely lay this change of plans at Professor Mean's door; were I destined to be a math star, I'd have made it far past the likes of him.

And leaving calculus showed me a different road. But my heart still aches a little for what I didn't learn in that class, in those pre-wildness years, the way you can rue a love you didn't marry. Everything went a little south for me after that, and I can't know if my failed affair with math had anything to do with it. But for me, calculus was the one that got away.

SINCE THE FIRST DAYS OF TYLER'S VISITS, THESE ARE some of the leaps of cognition she has made: She no longer thinks that Tula and Shiloh, the Belgian sheepdog who lives down the street, are sisters or, for that matter, my daughters. She understands that Peter and Pat—the humans who go along with Shiloh— actually have their own house, rather than the giant, amorphous dormitory for us all that she first imagined. After months of repeat explorations, she knows that my house—the *whole* house! as she exclaims—belongs to me and Tula, though she has claimed one upstairs room as her own.

She is figuring out the world, spatially and emotionally, with downhill ease, and whenever anything trips her up she gets frustrated. She hates to admit when she doesn't know something. If she is feeling stubborn, and I ask if she wants to know a word's meaning, she rolls her eyes and says, "I'm not really interested." Then she goes home and learns the word. Her vocabulary is random and enchanting: "preposterous," "willy-nilly." I try to mute how much I love her because she will wrinkle her nose or fling herself into the backyard with Tula. But she does tell me she wants a palomino mare when she grows up and plans to name her Gail.

"So, who was your first boyfriend?" Every week or two I am surprised by her leap into the unknown. But I always offer a version of the truth that will fit her expanding worldview. I tell her about a boy I liked when I was four or five, a shy kid named Mike, and she clearly knows I am patronizing her and wants the real thing. So I say, Well, when I was thirteen someone asked me to go steady. "Just *tell* me," she responds, which is her usual rejoinder when she is intrigued. "I said yes because I liked the color of his St. Christopher medal," I say. "That's what you got to wear if you were going steady with a boy. His St. Christopher was dark red.

"Then he kissed me at the local movie theater," I say, "and I immediately broke up with him." She wrinkles her nose in understanding and we both laugh demonically.

5

My social life in Lubbock was more fluid than my math pursuits and far more dangerous. I had always liked boys and had them as friends, and I went to a few rodeos and met some sweet guys and sat around drinking coffee with girls from the dorm. By the end of those two years I had a gentle, flower-child boyfriend with a long ponytail who rode a 750 Yamaha motorcycle. But there were a few skunks in the meadow before I found him. The first was a graduate student I'd met through a dorm-mate's boyfriend at the local coffee shop, and I was flattered by his attention—I was seventeen and he was handsome and a few years older, a serious student of English literature. Compared to the cowboys and business majors that covered Texas Tech's campus, this was exotic stuff. At the end of our date, he parked his car at the dark end of the dorm parking lot, lunged across the front seat and grabbed both my breasts, as though he were a blind calf in search of his mother. I was horrified. It was one of the least erotic gestures of my young life, and even in the midst of it he seemed like an idiot. I pushed him off and got out of the car. The memory makes me roll my eyes even now.

I was not so lucky in a later encounter, with a frat boy I'll call Jay, whom I had made the mistake of sleeping with one night in a determined effort to get over my first love. America was well into the sexual revolution by the late 1960s, but the Panhandle was not exactly Berkeley, and my relative innocence had yet to catch up with the headlines. I'd had sex only with my high school boyfriend, and two years after our breakup, I made the dispassionate choice to widen my horizon. The boy I picked was handsome, loud, fun, and forgettable. I went home to Amarillo for the summer and learned how to smoke dope, which did a much better job of horizon-widening. When I returned to Lubbock that fall, in what would be my last year there, I ran into Jay at a friend's off-campus apartment. He had been drinking and I had not; instead I'd had a few hits of Acapulco Gold, and was stoned enough to want to lie in a field and stare at the stars for the rest of my life.

Jay insisted I go for a ride with him so that we could talk. I had rebuffed his advances when I got back to town and I felt guilty; I assumed he wanted to convince me that we should try again. I also thought we could have this one conversation and be done. But in the car he fell silent and wouldn't say where we were going. We drove up to a dark little house, a place he said belonged to a friend, where he'd forgotten his jacket. We would only be a minute, he said. I was relieved to be out of the car and went with him inside. My clueless walk into the abattoir.

It was decades before I heard the term "date rape," and I remember thinking, at once, *Oh, that's what Jay did to me.* He threw me across the bed in the front room; I think he slapped me; I know he raped me. The assault was impersonal and mechanical. What I can still feel is my absolute stillness—the way I turned into a statue, inside and out. I remember staring at the ceiling and thinking, *Oh my God I'm so stoned, this is so horrible and I am so stoned.* I was infused with an out-of-body horror, more anger than fear, but outwardly, I was a cool customer. When he got off me I rearranged my clothes. I did nothing, said nothing, walked back to the car. He may have had a moment's chagrin, because he said quietly that he would take me back to the apartment where my friends were waiting.

Behind the wheel, though, his drunken rage—at himself? at me?—got the better of him. He started yelling and beating on the dashboard as he drove. Slut, whore, bitch, he called me; I had my hand on the door handle for the entire ride. When he pulled up to the apartment complex, he veered into a parking place and slammed on the brakes. I got out of the car and walked around to the driver's side, where his window was open. My voice was shaking. This was the first time I'd said a word.

"You no-good son-of-a . . ." I didn't get to finish. He leapt out of the car and threw me against the brick wall of the apartment building. He backhanded me, once, across the face, got in the car, and drove away. I had the bruise for a week.

What do I remember feeling about all this, so long ago? Disdain. Fury. Regret over my bad judgment— not that I had slept with someone, but that I had picked a whiskey-loving frat boy with no cool and no respect for women. That I had foolishly put myself in harm's way, because I'd gotten involved, for all the wrong reasons, with someone I didn't know well who turned out to be a violent loser.

For years I felt blessed that I had escaped any damaging aftermath from this experience. My outrage probably saved me from internalizing some of the classic trauma of sexual assault. But a subtler shift took place: the little erosions of faith that add up to wariness, or steely skepticism, or cynicism too tough to penetrate. It's an emotional runoff that happens over years and decades, and like any cultural norm it shapes you in immeasurable ways.

You can't read this story, or even write it, without thinking, *Did you tell, why didn't you tell, why didn't you call the police, why didn't you report it?*

It makes me sad now to realize that telling—anyone, any kind of protest—never occurred to me.

And when the woman told the story about being seated on a plane next to Trump in first class, where she said he grabbed her, when the woman in the bar remembered his hand up her skirt, when any number of women and girls recalled his storming the dressing rooms or throwing them against a wall, I thought, *Yeah, well, of course you didn't mention it.* We so rarely do. Or rather, did. "Honey, it's always been this way."

So no, I never thought to tell. I suppose you could say I hated the man for it, but mostly I tried to forget that night, and after a while I didn't think about him. There were a dozen ways to walk away from the memory, and I used them all. Smoked a lot of dope. Found a hippie boyfriend who loved women and made me laugh and gave me a blueprint for the next part of my life. It was easy to disdain the frat boys when you were poised on the brink of what seemed a revolution, and I was on my way to the den of iniquity, as my mother called it, in the counterculture hotbed of Austin. And so Date Rape Jay became part of a macho culture I was already fleeing—loutish men and empty plains, honed into an image of the past I could leave behind.

6

Two weeks after the election, and people are beginning to form in throngs on the street. I am raking leaves in the dark when Jim, my next-door neighbor, calls out, "Are you raking in the dark because you want to be left alone?" We laugh together, take solace in our shared inability to sleep. The people across the way gather in my driveway. The tools we're using to combat this collective despair are humor, Xanax, organizing. In January there will be a women's march in Washington; the sister march in Boston will have more than a million people on the street.

I live in a state that is historically progressive and Democratic, a college town whose self-definition is so urbane—sophistication bumping into smug—that its designation as "the People's Republic of Cambridge" is both earned and pejorative. But I grew up in the Bible Belt, spent the first nineteen years of my life in the midst of hardcore churchgoers and blindingly white conservatives. Whenever I returned there I learned how to go native, blend in like a lizard on a rock, listen to the heart and mind behind the right-wing politics or the born-again faith. It was important to me to do this, because it helped me connect with people and made me feel like I understood the character formed on those high plains. Maybe I was wrong; maybe I understood nothing. But the effort to identify opened me up. I have clung to this binocular vision, or tried to, through all the decades I've lived in the Northeast, believing it affords me emotional access to people I might otherwise judge, or separate myself from.

This time around, a different world. No one is laughing, or sparring; there are no good-natured efforts to agree to disagree. I have a long-scheduled appointment with my primary care physician, whom I have known for years. When I fill out the usual pre-visit forms, I note with new irony the standard annual screening for depression.

PLEASE CHECK ANY THAT APPLY:
❏ Have you been feeling anxious or desperate in the past two weeks?

❑ Have you had trouble sleeping?

❑ Have you had trouble engaging in your usual hobbies or activities?

Check, check, check, I wrote, with a little asterisk by each and a note: "post-election."

Dr. Ranere laughs when he sees my note. "You and everybody else," he says. He knows I'm in generally good health and my genetic draw is pretty straightforward; if alcoholism or suicide doesn't get you in my family, you tend to live for a long time. My problems are orthopedic and what my therapist calls little-d depression. I take my vitamin-Z Zoloft to seal off the basement door, surround myself with dogs, walk and row and swim to stave off arthritis and the late effects of the polio I had as an infant. If I'm not limping or sad, I'm in pretty good shape. I am not, for instance, sticking my head in the oven, like my Uncle Roy did after leaving a seven-page suicide note. I've avoided shock treatments, four lousy marriages, bankruptcy, and the chlorine gas of World War I—all of which happened to relatives on both sides of the gene pool. So when I calculate the odds, I did all right. I had my last drink to date more than thirty years ago. That's really something.

I suppose you could say that, after all the ordinary

pushing and shoving of life, I am an educated, self-sufficient feminist and registered Democrat who gives her money to liberal causes, subscribes to three newspapers, and is not afraid of bullies. Multiplied by many million, I am Donald Trump's worst nightmare.

TYLER IS LEARNING HOW TO READ, THOUGH SHE doesn't realize it yet. I see it when she calls her mother from my landline and sounds out the numbers and letters on the keypad. One day after she hangs up I hear her say "OFF" as she presses the button, and I say, "You can read!" And she says, amazed, "I *can*?" as though I have told her she can fly. She has not yet made the magical leap where she knows what she knows, and so reading—the thought of it—still occupies a mysterious place in the future. But her grasping what she has done is powerful mojo, a hint of what lies ahead. Today, "OFF." Tomorrow, Proust.

I teach her to type on my mother's old Royal manual typewriter, a thirty-five-pound hunk of steel built in the 1940s that she made her living with for years. I learned to type on it when I was fourteen or fifteen, and the smell of the ink and the carriage's *ding* elicit an out-of-time pleasure—I like the notion of several generations pounding this machine. Tyler sits at the typewriter and gazes off into space with her finger on her chin, as though impersonating a moody, thoughtful writer.

Then she types wildly, jamming the keys, mostly garble but occasionally words: TULA, Tyler. "How do you spell 'Shiloh,'" she calls, and I realize she's going for broke. Then one day she gets a full sentence. "Tyler GOEZ TO se GAIL AND TULA." She rips the paper from the carriage and thrusts it toward me, and says, "Now you will *never* forget me!"

The whole operation happens fast, this leap into consciousness and language. One day she finds a book I wrote and sees my photo on the back cover, and turns to me, astonished. "You wrote all these words?" she says, eyes big, and I see her glimpse the truth at the brink of literacy: that an entire treasure chest of language exists, and that one might actually have that much to say.

In the next few months she decides she will be a writer when she grows up. Every few weeks she asks how the book is coming that she knows she is in, and before I have a chance to answer she tells me about her book—or books, as she is writing several at once. We have what I call joint editing sessions, which really involve roaming around between fantasy and reality. We lie on the living room floor and make up stories. I borrow from old favorites—Mrs. Piggle-Wiggle, for instance, where the kids walked on the ceilings of the house. But mostly I listen. Tyler's plots are Byzantine and free-associative, and I occasionally rein her in with questions or plot suggestions. This week I've been hearing the adventures of a young girl named Kayla and her hapless family, involving several car accidents, crutches, and sleepovers. Finally, bored with the demands of fiction and her laborious plot, Tyler leaps to her feet and uses her outstretched hands to make the point. "TIME PASSES."

So with that stage direction, Kayla's baby brother is grown: His sleepovers have turned into fatherhood in the blink of an eye. But what happened to Kayla? I ask. I'm interested, but I'm also trying to give Tyler some subtle instruction on finishing thoughts. If she wants to be a writer, she has to follow her tumbleweeds down every trail she invents.

"Kayla lives alone," she announces. "She has a farm with lots of animals—goats and sheep, three horses, chickens, a German shepherd, and two border collies. She makes apple pie and can eat it whenever she wants. And she has a pool the length of a park! And she can swim in the snow at night.

"Her house is full of peace and quiet and she has a fantastic life."

7

Austin, Texas, 1970

O ne morning on the way to Latin class, I found $7 lying on the grassy mall. My heart fluttered when I saw the money, and I reached to pick it up. I needed it for the illegal abortion I was having in a couple of weeks. I was nineteen and six weeks pregnant and not in love, and my ex-boyfriend and I were planning to drive to Mexico, where you could get the procedure done for $160. We had agreed to split the cost. To get my share, I had been going without lunch and typing student term papers for $10 apiece. Now, with the $7, I was halfway there.

I had moved to Austin several months earlier, and met a tall, soft-voiced fellow who had just returned from studying French literature at the Sorbonne. We smoked dope together and sat on the grounds of the capitol listening to music and speeches about smashing imperialism, and evenings we would go back to his place and make gentle, not-very-interesting love to the background swoon of the Moody Blues. He introduced me to Sartre and sometimes mumbled to me in French during sex, which thrilled me but only for a while. He was mellow but controlling—a lethal combination I spotted pretty quickly. I had plenty of half-doomed relationships still ahead of me, but even then I knew the satin-voiced version of prison was not for me. Within a few months, we would each move on to other gardens—he to a pretty hippie girl with long braids and a quiet demeanor, I to my first women's liberation rally.

But a couple of weeks after we'd broken up, my period was late: The bright, somehow affirming blood flow didn't show. "I'm late." That was how we put it back then, and I doubt any two words were as frightening to a young woman of that time and place, when the future unfurled with some promise and some risk but certainly alternatives to the shotgun marriages of our mothers. "I'm late" was the female equivalent of being 1-A—your future revealed with a draft notice or a pregnancy test done at a doctor's office with the attendant tight-lipped judgment. We were three years away from *Roe v. Wade,* and if somewhere in the glistening years of youth you didn't get your period, the options were draconian: become a mother when you were still a child, carry to term and give the baby up for adoption, or risk your life in an illegal, difficult-to-find medical procedure. I chose the last.

Birth control was hardly the buffet of choices it would soon become. A year earlier, in Amarillo for the summer, I'd gotten a prescription for the pill after being coached by friends. First I made an appointment with the doctor whose name I'd been given. The code phrase to use with the receptionist was "family planning." Then I went to Woolworth to buy a fake engagement ring. On the day of the appointment I donned the ring along with heels and stockings and marched into his office. It was clear there would be no exam. I sat across from a grim-faced doctor, and my voice shook while I talked too fast about my imaginary fiancé. I knew he didn't believe me, and that it didn't matter. He was tight-lipped and refused to meet my eyes when he handed me the scrip. I felt embarrassed by his discomfort, and I made up for it by thanking him excessively.

The early birth control pills had three times the estrogen of later replacements, and the side effects were awful. I threw up every morning the first week and put on ten pounds in a month. By the time I'd moved to Austin and started dating the French major, I'd given up the pill, relying on condoms and denial for protection. And before the skipped period that changed everything, I had been scheduled for an appointment at university health services to figure out my options.

The ex had shown his character when I told him I was pregnant, though I was already done with him by then and didn't expect much else. He seemed impatient and guilty, as though I had visited this plague upon him and it was bound to be an enormous hassle. He was from a wealthy family, and when I told him all I needed was half the money for an abortion, he didn't even try to hide his relief.

I lived at an off-campus dorm where I was paired with a soft-spoken roommate named Kirsten, and I woke up one day and felt the tenderness of swollen breasts and thought *oh God no* and then I was flooded with nausea. Kirsten heard me gagging in the bathroom before breakfast, so I told her. She was concerned and no-nonsense, rational in the face of my crisis, and she knew what to do. She called her boyfriend, who had been through this a year earlier with his former girlfriend. Chris was fluent in Spanish and a sweet, thoughtful guy, and he jumped into action. There was a doctor in Reynosa, Mexico, he told me, a female physician who financed her clinic by performing abortions on *norteamericana* girls like me. No back-alley coat-hanger job like what you got in the States. Chris made the call and set the date, and within a couple of days we had a plan.

. . .

About five hours south of Austin, Reynosa is a border town in northern Mexico. Back then it was a sleepy place, with a small *mercado* and street-side cafés. Kirsten and Chris were driving me, and we wanted to get there and back in the same day, in case I needed medical care in the States. My ex, dutiful but cold, insisted on going, and though I didn't particularly want him along, I was too tired and scared to argue.

The four of us made the trip down in rock-hard silence. My fear when I revisit it now was hard, too—a stony numbness, some place outside of time. A strong resolve and no tears. The overriding thing I remember was the desolation of the road going by as we sped south—I was in the back seat, and I spent most of the time staring out the window.

The waiting room at the clinic was crowded with patients. We were the only Americans, and I was sure the other patients knew why I was there. A few people looked toward me and then turned away, a gesture that seemed more sad than judgmental. Such is the ego-centrism of youth: the assumption that these people paid much mind to the young *gringa* in their midst. We waited a long time to see the doctor, a weary-looking, courteous woman in her forties. Chris translated the instructions she gave us. She handed me prescriptions for antibiotics and muscle relaxants, which must have been a pre-op anesthetic, gave me directions on where to go and how to take them. She told me to come back in two hours.

We walked across the square to *la farmacia* to get the pills. The man behind the counter smiled when he handed me the bag, and not in a nice way. I was startled; in those days, Mexican pharmacies were pretty much unregulated; you could order amphetamines or tranquilizers as easily as aspirin. I got a Coke to swallow the dose of pills, and we walked over to an outdoor café to kill the time.

And then the drugs must have taken effect, because I remember only one scene from the next several hours. I am on my back on a hospital bed in a spare, clean room with a single lightbulb overhead. The doctor is in the corner, and she calls over a girl—fifteen or sixteen—to stand next to me. The girl is very pretty, with enormous eyes, and I take her hand. *"Hija?"* I say, for daughter, and she smiles and nods. Then everything goes dark.

We left the clinic sometime later. It was night and I was lying in the back seat of the car, and Kirsten nudged me awake as we approached the long line at U.S. Customs. Our car was pulled over and all the doors thrown open. The agents told me to get out of the car, and I was taken inside a room at the customs building, where a female agent strip-searched me. I was half-asleep and off-balance and weak, and I held on to the wall during the search so that I wouldn't fall. I was still bleeding. No one asked me anything. I had enough Spanish to understand a little of the mocking conversation going on among the border guards. They'd targeted me because the pharmacist had called ahead to alert them.

They took away the painkillers I'd been given and eventually let us go. I was too doped up to care much while any of this was happening, or to be outraged by it later—it seemed merely one in a line of indignities that went with being a sexually active young woman in 1970. We got back to Austin around midnight, and I slept for ten hours. The next day I walked over to student health services to be checked out, the place where I'd verified that I was pregnant. The doctor who saw me was a low-key man in his forties. When he finished the exam, he came around the table and patted me on the shoulder. He said, "Whoever did this did a good job."

After I finished at the health center I walked over to the Nighthawk, a local restaurant on Nineteenth Street that bordered the UT campus and had the comfort of good food and leather booths. I sat in a booth and ordered coffee with milk, a large Coke, and a chicken dinner that could feed a football player. Then I walked out into the Texas sunshine, well and home, and my eyes teared with thanks for the bright, precious thing that was my life. A few weeks later, I was fitted for an IUD.

Sometime the following spring I wandered into my first women's liberation rally, part of a tectonic shift that helped haul the Western world into the modern age. I was a white woman of privilege—a middle-class background in America, for starts, and the beginning of a college education—but I wasn't immune to the common cruelties of a society where women could still be treated as property or as biblical Jezebels. At nineteen, with good intentions and above-average intelligence, I had a fairly ordinary and entitled life. Here is part of what was ordinary: Already I had encountered academic favoritism (Professor Mean) and sexual harassment (in a summer job in Amarillo, the boss offered me $1,000 to sleep with him, then threatened to fire me when I said no). I had been "taken advantage of," which is what they used to call date rape, and then assaulted by a frat boy I'd dated. I'd been told that women made lousy lawyers (not aggressive or articulate enough), that "chicks" who took a stance against the

Vietnam War were "just looking to get laid," that, in fact, getting laid was what we were good for—the start of a long, monochromatic path of motherhood and marital servitude. All these messages were direct but impersonal, embedded tenets that even the smartest or most defiant girl could not ignore.

Until we did, which was the first part of the battle. The women I met and allied myself with over the next several years were talented and wild and far more complex than any orthodox definition of who I'd been told women were, and that realization widened the sky and made every day feel like street theater. We threw ourselves across doorways and stormed stages and committed colorful acts of sabotage, but our greatest strategic victory was something interior: the shift when we stopped caring so much what men thought, or presumed, or demanded. When we turned our attention away from the status quo and toward one another.

This sounds naïve, or idealistic, and of course it was both and had to be at that age. Our vision and momentum were enough to create a carnival universe over the next decade: a couple of women's theater groups and organic farms, a community of prophets and sinners who slept together or didn't but who were loyal to the tribe first and foremost. We felt we deserved everything, and if it didn't exist we made it up: Womenspace, the

Fly by Night Printing Collective, the Soeur Queens. When we needed to sound legitimate we invented a name: the Women's Cultural Arts Association, I think we called it, which didn't accomplish much but looked good on letterhead.

Austin was an easy place to survive back then, and if you weren't careful the milk-and-honey mecca could turn to quicksand. A lot of us leapt, or left, and the places we landed bore the scars and signatures of what it had taken to get there. Some women became mothers, some went to medical or law school or became musicians or activists. For me it meant that I got the nerve to return to graduate school, then pack the car with a typewriter and a couple of bottles of whiskey and head for the East Coast. The casualty list was also long—depression and substance abuse and rotten luck—and I used to think that meant something, something about tragic heroines and ultra-dramatic personae, but now I think it just has to do with life, with trying to stay the course. Watch enough decades go by and every path has broken stones along the way.

History is a series of snapshots, sweet or tattered images that shift through the years to haunt us, to give ballast to the entire story. And however much we waste time and heart imagining what might have been, the truth is that it's impossible, really, to examine an unlived life. What we feel instead, I think, is the failed dream. Sometimes fantasy is merely a necessary lie—what gives breathing room to fact, to make the present bearable.

I know some of the memories are sepia-toned and suspect. At some point you shuffle the cards and call the deck a life. Maybe we were just young and beautiful fools, sitting around smoking and drinking and scripting psychodrama, avoiding the blueprint for growing up. I do know this: The women's movement gave me a reclamation of self I had found nowhere else, and I don't like imagining my life without it.

Here's how the story might have turned out, in the alternative universe of pregnant at nineteen, year 1970, keeps baby.

—I marry the French major, reluctantly on both our parts, and divorce within a couple of years.
—Or: I leave college and move back to the Texas Panhandle, where my heartbroken parents help me in silent rage. Maybe I get a small apartment, a secretarial job; maybe I take night classes at the local junior college.

In either case I probably drink too much, become cynical and depressed. The next decade or two would be a mix of blind maternal love, exhaustion, and resentment for the freedom I had lost. For the open-ended paragraph of youth.

Each scenario makes me flinch: They all star a child I bear who suffers from my emotional immaturity, who needs more of everything than I had at that age. That's the worst part, of course: one accidental pregnancy, two casualties.

And now: Did I ever second-guess my decision, after that day and night in Reynosa? Suffer any regrets, my biological clock trilling its alarm at what I had done? No—not ever, not at all.

For the first time in many years, though, I've thought about the other people in this story.

—My roommate and her boyfriend, whom I'd met only once or twice. They didn't know me well; we were all so young. And yet they knew what to do, and more important, were willing to do it, which included shepherding a pregnant woman across international borders for an illegal medical procedure.

—The customs agent, who conducted her cold strip-search on a young woman who was doped up and bleeding. Was the agent a devout Catholic, a mother, someone who could have ever been in a similar jam? Did she resent me, despise me, want to take a swing at my reckless, white-girl attitude? Or maybe she was just trying to keep her job. Be one of the boys.

—The woman doctor, whom I remember as patient and tired. What kind of a struggle was it, religiously or ethically, to do what she did? She treated me with dignity, and I assume she was the same with her other patients, people from town and pregnant girls from the States. What that cost her is something I cannot know. *Whoever did this did a good job.*

Then there was the beautiful girl, *ángel, hija,* standing next to me at the operating table while I went under. She is probably a grandmother now. I wish I could thank them both.

For decades, the routine intake for a standard medical exam has included a two-part question, with a blank space for the patient to fill in a number:

Pregnancies: _____ . Carried to term: _____ .

The question is a euphemistic protocol, and takes care of the messy business of writing, say, "miscarriage," "abortion," "trips to Reynosa." Abortion in some places is still a scarlet "A." "Carried to term—zero" covers several possibilities. It is designed to inquire about your body and what it's been through, not your soul.

When I went in for a recent annual checkup, a new nurse practitioner ran through a medical history with me. She was a large, confident woman around forty, and I liked her immediately. We went through the questions staccato-style. Ex-smoker? Yes, quit at forty. Exercise regularly? Yes. Parents deceased, one sibling, living? Yes, and yes. One pregnancy, terminated?

"Yes," I said, and then, without thinking, "I was nineteen."

"Good choice," she said, without looking up, and we moved on down the page.

It was an unguarded moment, and later I thought about what it had taken for us to have that exchange—the straightforward ease of it. Without her warmth and our initial connection, I wouldn't have bothered to say what I did ("I was nineteen"). Had I been more reserved, I expect she'd have stayed silent. Instead we had reached across decades and generations, and agreed, without any fuss, to agree on this one thing. Good choice.

That afternoon I went for a row on the Charles. I left the boathouse tired and happy, and, pulling out of the parking lot, I saw a group of girls from the high school on their way into the club for crew practice. A main thoroughfare runs alongside the river, and they were wending their way through stopped traffic, laughing together, indifferent to the cars around them. They were seniors, probably, and watching them I thought about the heedless beauty that horses have when they move—all that energy possessing space. These young almost-women had the same grace. They deserved this world; they were moving through it unaware, and soon they would be on the river, taking a thousand-pound boat across flat water. I loved their arrogance. I loved what they didn't yet know.

T YLER IS BRUSHING THE DOG'S TEETH, A TASK THAT Tula cheerfully endures, while I stand at the sink washing dishes. It's a late-summer day, the weeks between her camp and the start of school, and all our conversations have the laze of uninterrupted dialogue. Out of the blue she says, over my shoulder, "So—did you vow never to marry?"

I stifle a laugh. Where did she get this bodice-ripper phrase? She is too young for *Jane Eyre*. But her questions are always serious and I meet this one head-on. "Well, I didn't find the one absolutely right person," I tell her. "So I spread my love around. I've loved a lot of people, and animals."

She seems to accept this as a good enough answer, as do I, on most days. I don't say, as she often does, "Well, it's complicated."

I do not say, *When you are a young revolutionary who believes marriage is a bourgeois institution that enslaves women and empowers the state, it's tricky finding the right guy to hang out with.* I don't say, *Oh, well, there was him, and then him, and then her, and then him, and then I left Texas and it all started again. Him, and him, and her, and then, eventually . . . just . . . me.*

I don't tell her about the letters I found this week, between me and a lover, written thirty-five years ago. "I would destroy you," R. wrote me, fearing, I think, that the darkness he saw in himself would overshadow us both. And later, in the same letter, "Go write the Great American Novel." He didn't, and I didn't either, though some part of me knew to leave—to get away from him and Texas and every toxic element there, including me, that was trying to take me out. More than a decade later, off his meds and wandering Europe in despair, he checked into a hotel in Copenhagen and took an overdose of pills. There was no note.

I don't tell her about the time he asked me to be a drug mule from Lima to Miami so we could make our fortune, and that I nearly said yes but changed my mind at the last minute—that some deep core part of me said *Don't be this stupid—it's a nosedive from twenty thousand feet.* And he went anyway and someone else got arrested. He called me three weeks later, in Taos, and cried and said he loved me and begged me to come back to Texas. By then I was living in a yurt with a woman I thought would get me over men. I didn't go home, and later, when I did, we pretended the phone call hadn't happened.

I don't say, *Oh, Tyler, life is so long and so complicated and sometimes it's just biology. And there are tragedies and pratfalls and blind alleys around every corner.*

I don't say, *Well, honey, I had a tendency to fall for the bad ones. Sometimes I left and sometimes they did. Oh yes and also, I was married to Johnnie Walker Red for a couple of decades, and when you're in love with a bottle it tends to crowd the room.*

But all of those omissions are just facts, unorganized, so the most important thing I do not tell her, not yet, is that the mistakes, if you're lucky, can become tributaries to somewhere else. You look up and all the choices you made and the U-turns and the wanderlust—they settle into a life with its own metronome and internal logic. We wed ourselves to whatever narrative we have. This is called acceptance, or denial, and is a central underpinning of most world religions.

When I found that letter from R. this week I cried, but a part of me was skeptical even as I watched my young heart pining. Why that particular letter, read on that day? It was one of a hundred, saved and forgotten. This is a problem of material culture, or memory, or the junction between the two: Whatever makes it through thirty or forty years into the archive can supersede the memory, can take on the sometimes unearned weight of being The Past. When in fact it's only a bit of the past, a scribbled-on matchbook cover in the scheme of things, one photo saved instead of the four lost or discarded, one more lover who went the way of the dustbin of history. The collision of time and space: Presto, the story of the universe. Of one ordinary woman.

What Tyler is too young to understand, what I believe but forget most of the time, is that the heart is a dowsing tool and finds where it needs to go. However much I can feel trapped by self-inflicted isolation, I have to acknowledge that I walked straight into this life, half trotted, arms swinging and eyes open. I made decisions that got me here. I sought and seem to require a house with an enormous chair, with dogs and an open-door policy but no full-time humans, not so far, and I'm in my seventh decade so that's a pretty long so-far. This awareness can be a crushing burden in the dead of winter, or when I am injured, say, or forgot to buy broccoli, or don't want to go to a party meant to be fun but that seems onerous. It's a problem of the soul and psyche, not food or shelter, and when I remember that, I must also remember that no one is protected from consciousness itself, the ability to want and dream and suffer and regret. Nobody gets a cakewalk.

I think about this when the dog and I walk the winter streets at night and I see the amber glow from inside the houses, where the other people's stories, the perfect ones, are being lived. There is so much we cannot see.

The book Tyler and I are supposedly writing is a fantasy that wafts in and out of consciousness, depending upon the summer days and basketball at the park and whether or not, say, we have decided to run hurdles or make pie. For a couple of years we've invented a multitude of stories involving hundred-pound cats in the basement, magic potions made from cinnamon, horses that can fly. But the older she gets, the more realism rears its head. One day she appears with a thick spiral notebook, climbs onto the stool at the kitchen counter, and writes on the first page: "TYLER AND GAIL: THE ADVENTURE BEGINS."

8

J oan had gone her own way in Dallas. The ride we'd picked up in Albuquerque had taken us that far south and dropped us where the highways diverged, and now it was late on a Sunday night and cold for a Texas winter and I still had two hundred miles to go. I was trying to get to Austin, where I lived in a house with five adults and four dogs and where things were so lax that nobody would notice if I went missing for a day or even a week. We were all hippies and musicians and vegetarians; no one had any money or a car that worked, and hitchhiking was the preferred mode of travel: spontaneous and free.

Texas was known for spending more money on its highways than on education, but I remember that stretch of road as dark and uninviting. I was wearing jeans and a rough-out jacket with a high sheepskin collar, and after I'd found a good hitching spot and unloaded my pack, I pulled my hair into a ponytail and tucked it inside my jacket. Then I stuck out my thumb, the classic half-semaphore wave with a backward half-jog. I was hoping that I looked like a young guy.

The first car I waved on because I didn't like the look of the driver. Another twenty minutes passed before anyone stopped. Then an old Chevy pulled up. The driver was about thirty, with slicked-back hair. He looked startled when I opened the door. "Oh hey!" he said, "I thought you were a dude. Where are you headed?"

Our trip had started a couple of weeks earlier, when Joan and I had set out from Austin for Aspen, Colorado, a thousand miles northwest, and made it almost straight through with a harrowing midnight ride over Independence Pass. We had gone to visit an old boyfriend of mine who had turned ski bum, and when we got to Aspen at one A.M. he didn't even seem surprised. Such was the mañana culture of those days, when everything mattered but not for long, and we all thought we were Neal Cassady or Rosalie Sorrels, when really we were just young and daredevil-dumb and lucky to get through it all alive.

We had come back through Taos and hung out for

a few days and dodged a couple of weirdos and laughed our way through to central Texas on our way home. That was the thing about time-space travel: If you could stay on the bull, keep riding the light beam, the mind and heart were so full that you didn't have to think about the crash.

The man who stopped for me on the road outside Dallas was James Dean cool, probably hip before hippies existed, and I liked his looks and the fact that he'd thought I was male. I threw my pack in the back seat and got in.

He was going all the way to Austin. By now it was late, maybe nine or ten P.M., and we had four hours ahead of us and I was glad to have gotten a ride straight through. He asked me a couple of questions about where I'd been but was mostly quiet. Those first few minutes of a ride were always crucial, when the driver and the hitchhiker made tacit assessments of each other. And hitching solo was a game changer, which is why I'd gone camouflage before putting my thumb out. You might get a ranter who doesn't think you should be hitching, or another hippie who has grass to share. This man was mellow and respectful, and after a few minutes I settled in. Then he glanced over at me and started to reach under the seat.

My heart clenched and I don't think I thought

anything at all except that I was helpless and had no idea what was about to happen. He pulled a long butcher or hunting knife out from under his right foot and showed me the blade, his face expressionless. He paused for a second, then said, "I keep this with me when I pick up hitchhikers so that I can protect myself." Then he placed it back where it had been.

I had broken out in a sweat when he reached under the seat. Now I sat back and looked ahead and waited for my heart to slow, and he turned on the radio, low. "You like country?" He spoke with a hint of apology in his voice.

"I do," I said, nodding. We drove.

I knew from the tone of his voice and his careful gesture that he was not threatening me—he was drawing a line in the sand. Watching out for any kind of crazy that might be on the road, and telling them at the start of the ride not to mess with him. I doubt he ever used that knife. And it turned out to be one of the easier rides I ever had. Maybe he softened because he hadn't wanted to scare me, just alert me, but we talked, on and off, all the way to Austin. He told me he had a young daughter with Down syndrome whom he loved more than anything. We shared a couple of beers, when drinking behind the wheel was still legal in Texas. I wasn't in trouble with alcohol yet, could still have a beer and not have it turn into ten. By the time we saw the lights of Austin it was after one A.M. He was going across town, but he drove me to my door.

A block from home I remember thinking *Oh shit, is this where the payoff comes?* because he'd been so kind, and now he had driven me home and would probably try to cop a feel, even with his beautiful daughter and beautiful story. But no, I got none of that. He shook my hand and wished me luck and said to be careful. Before he drove away, he told me that his name was Tony.

I like remembering that story, because it didn't always end so well and because the world is full of so much meanness and posturing and people pretending to be somebody else. But Tony had not a shred of pretense about him. He was exactly who he seemed to be from the moment he pulled over on that Texas night.

The time it didn't end so well was a couple of years later, another lonely stretch from Austin to Taos. I had been living in San Francisco and had left there in early autumn, traveling with a friend from California. We'd been on the road a long time. Katie was a small, wiry car mechanic who'd grown up in New York; she had a black belt in kung fu and was sensible and strong. Now we were trying to get a ride through the bleaker reaches of the Texas Panhandle, near Muleshoe and Dimmitt, on our way to the interstate. We were tired by then and we broke a rule of the women hitchhiker's code: Never get in a car that passes you, hesitates, and turns around to come back and get you. A bad sign.

Second rule we broke: Don't get in a car with a lone man who doesn't remove his sunglasses to talk to you. (Who made these rules? They seem brilliant, in retrospect.)

It was cold and getting late. We wanted to cross the Texas border and make it to Albuquerque. The man was around thirty, white, all smiles, and when he learned we were going to New Mexico said he could get us to the highway.

I got in the front seat and began another strategic piece of the hitchhiker's convention: Draw out the driver. Be friendly. Ask a lot of questions. He told me he was stationed at a nearby air force base, and I relaxed a little. He mentioned his fiancée and where they had spent a holiday. It seemed like it was going to be OK.

About ten minutes later he put on his left-turn signal and abruptly turned onto a farm-to-market road.

"You're going the wrong way," I said.

"I know a shortcut," he said.

Farm-to-market roads are what they sound like: rural routes, usually paved two-lane roads that allow farmers and ranchers to get to town. They can be desolate stretches, particularly out where we were, territory where I had gone dove hunting with my dad when I was a girl. Jesus. This time we were the doves.

Probably because of the cardboard-flat terrain in north Texas, most farm roads have a deep, sharply angled bank as the only pullover. The pitch of the bank allows runoff from rain, but it's more like a ditch than a road lane, less visible than a normal breakdown lane and a lot less friendly.

What happened next happened fast, and all of it on my part was instinct and adrenaline.

He sped up once he was on the farm-to-market road, and had gotten a mile or so from the highway. By the time he pulled over into the ditch I had my door open and one foot out. And now he took off his sunglasses and smiled at me. "I've paid my deposit," he said. "Now it's time for you to pay your dues."

In the braggadocio of crisis, I remember thinking *Oh God, what a stupid thing to say.* He said it awkwardly, as though he had rehearsed this moment and his role in it, rehearsed being menacing and convincing. A punk on a dirt road who could ruin it all.

I have no recollection of getting out of the car, though I remember yelling to Katie, *Get the packs.* And somehow I am standing at the rear of his car, shaking with fury, shouting out the numbers on his license plate. He is out of the car, too, by his door, arguing with me, sounding both whiny and ominous. Katie is frozen by the side of the road.

"I have your license plate," I yell. "I know where you're stationed, and who your commanding officer is. I know your fiancée's name, and where your parents live. Your life is *over* if you do this." I speak with the certainty of Atticus Finch, when in fact I am crazy with fear, a slight twenty-two-year-old in the middle of nowhere, with a friend even smaller than I who has yet to say a word.

He is pleading with me not to tell. He is a monster, unmasked. He offers to drive us back to the main road.

I'm sorry, he says. I didn't—please get in the car. I thought—

Katie looks at me confused. "Maybe we should get a ride to the highway," she says, in a timid, foggy voice, and I realize then that she is no help at all, that she has gone still like a trapped bird, and I start to yell at the man again. "If you're not out of sight in thirty seconds I'm calling your CO. *GET BACK IN YOUR CAR AND GO.*"

And then he is gone. That dry Panhandle road catching the last dust and whorls of his tires, spinning as he takes off.

My heart is pounding and I have the energy of a firefighter. I have been a first responder to my own catastrophe. We walk in silence, lugging packs, about twenty minutes to the highway. I keep thinking that throughout my tirade, I had in mind the notion that Katie was a martial arts master. That beyond my anger was her muscle. Finally I say, "So—do you think you could have taken him?"

She stops walking and looks at me and I see it in her eyes: It has not occurred to her until now that she could have done anything. She has forgotten all about the black belt, prowess eclipsed by fear, years of effort undone by one asshole on an empty Texas road. She looks ashamed, and her pain is enraging; now I want to kill him even more. He robbed something from her that day, and I hope she got it back. But I don't know that she did.

This story should end with my saying I never hitched again, I learned my lesson, I took kung fu, I got a gun. None of which happened, though I did learn to fire a gun, and have an old copy of *The Women's Gun Pamphlet*, published by an underground press in 1975, that's a rough-hewn documentation of how pissed off and desperate a lot of women were in those days. But over the next few years I stopped hitching and started giving women rides, usually straight to wherever they were going, and I told them I'd nearly been raped or maybe killed and to be careful and please stop getting into cars with strangers.

My orbit of rebellion had begun as a moody, alienated teenager, found a home for a while as an anti-war hippie girl, and somewhere in there a streak of wildness and rage emerged. Now I think wildness is a cover for all kinds of pain, though I hadn't a hint of the connection then. Everyone I knew was flirting with some kind of disaster; between hallucinogens and Vietnam and riots in the street, the decade offered a smorgasbord of ways to fuck you up. I was making my way through some dark tunnels. That's the piece of it now, nearly a half century later, that puzzles and intrigues me. The overlap between the personal story and the social mores. The normal boundary tests of adolescence, gone over the cliff.

At what point does ordinary rebellion become callous disregard? It would be years before I recognized this passage as anything but common, years before I realized, with solemn alarm, how close I had come to blowing it all in a dozen ways. My mother had given me the usual instructions on proper, ladylike behavior; my dad had lorded it over the boys in the 'hood when they came calling. We were in many ways a typical postwar nuclear family, my parents struggling for a better life in what to them was the big city of Amarillo. We had the common allotment of joys and boredom and failures, no trouble large enough to launch the projectile of peril I became. I can hear my dad raging at me that I was killing my mother; I see my mother's stone-silent sadness—both memories from the summer I got arrested on a marijuana charge that was ultimately thrown out. But their condemnation only fueled my anger, made me haughty with self-righteousness and pawing at the ground to get out. Why didn't I comprehend, even a little, the fragility of life? So when I look back now at that girl with her thumb out, zip-lining her way into trouble and then yelling her way out, I feel the way my mother must have felt: sad but helpless. Glad she lived, sorry she was confused enough to almost not.

I keep thinking of the old peach-colored Take Back the Night T-shirt, circa 1977, that I wore until it fell apart. That's the tangible object here. A piece of the mosaic that goes from Danger Girl to feminist hipster to—let's just save our own damn life. Maybe it was a matter of brain development, that prefrontal cortex finally learning how not to bungee-jump toward hell. But I think it was a societal evolution, too, from self-destruction to taking back the night to a reclamation of the soul.

I have a mental snapshot of a night in Austin during the early days of the women's movement when a lot of us had congregated at a neighborhood house. We called the place Robinson Street, because that's where it was, but it was code for boots off, feet up, beer in the fridge. "Meet you at Robinson Street." "Everyone's at Robinson Street." Anti-war strategy in one corner, a poker game in the other. Why were things so much fun then? Some women were in love with each other, some not, all of us inhaling a freedom that we'd discovered in the overthrow of bourgeois expectations.

The phone rang. The woman who answered listened for a minute, raised an eyebrow, and called my name. It was a man I'd been sleeping with for a few months, wanting to know when I was coming home. I was standing in the kitchen holding a long-corded wall phone, listening to him complain, and looking out at the women in the other room. And I remember thinking, almost wistfully, *If you were a lesbian you wouldn't ever have to go home.* Meaning that the party was here, that home was where I already was, that I wouldn't have to report back to barracks, ever.

That was more than four decades ago, and even now I can feel the mix of confusion and intrigue I had, like a child figuring out a math problem. I had bumped up against an insight that would change things for me, alter the universe just a little: the realization that men were too often the arbiters of everything, the authority we answered to, or gave our cardboard swords at the end of the day.

This was not simply a sexual or romantic epiphany. It was wider than that, and the fact that I remember it—remember the evening summer glow from the next room, the yellow phone, the man's voice—is evidence of its value in the course my life took. It was a moment when I began to recognize that I got to be in charge of my own freedom. Years passed while I fine-tuned that idea, made it something about independence and self-respect instead of merely rebellion. But the light that night—the laughter and autonomy and affection in that houseful of women—became the ideal notion of shelter and adventure, of what life ought to be.

There would be other such moments in the years to come, the start of a path taken or a door closed, an interior voice saying *No, I won't do that. No, not for me, don't think so.* It makes me sad to realize this now because part of aging is the rue and reach of the past. But also glad that I was looking out for myself, though as with most pieces of wisdom I didn't know that for years, and it didn't always feel so hot at the time.

The No-not-for-mes covered a lot of ground: men and women I left, graduate programs I didn't finish, jobs and cities I fled. Was all of it running? Not at all, in retrospect, though sometimes it felt as though it was—so much of being young is living with liberation and fear entwined. I was always going toward, even when the toward was milky or unknown. Curiosity beat out fear by a millimeter, every time, and sometimes only by that. I left the man who shattered my happy autonomy that night at Robinson Street; I left the woman I had loved a few years later; I ran to and then abandoned the graduate program that honed my mind as sharply as feminism had honed my heart. Through it all I clung to whiskey to give me courage, which worked marvelously until it didn't, and its failure was the size of a crevasse, monstrous and deep and the biggest danger of them all.

9

So yes, Tyler, there are so many things I do not tell you. Things I don't really think about in full, not in linked-together sentences and years that constitute a narrative. But your easy, beautiful questions have made me consider them, the stories of a life, viewed differently from the treehouse that is aging.

For instance: Why *did* I never marry? More men than women have asked me this question over the years, and my answer is usually shorthand, a euphemistic shrug. Why did I leave him, and then her, why did I pray for a mate but run from the ones who presented themselves? "You're the least desperate single woman I know," a friend said to me thirty years ago, when we were both young and working in a newsroom. I didn't understand her comment. What was there to be desperate about, particularly if you didn't want kids and were financially solvent? More to her point: I had felt desperate inside of love, not when I was free of it. Free of it was like, *Thank you God I survived that, oh look here is my sword and here's my self-worth, right where I left them, never gonna do that again.* I was not so great at love, not the big ones, anyway, and I was very good at being alone. Maybe it was bad luck or bad choices, or something broken inside of me. Some of it may have had to do with growing up on those empty plains, where days could be so uneventful that I used to lie in the grass and try to catch the flowers growing. A childhood like that teaches you the resources of your own company.

Shards of a journal, kept in the early 1970s, when I was living in Northern California and then wandering the southwestern coast of Mexico, below Guadalajara. It was just after the summer I had slept with a woman for the first time, a delicate, sensual affair that happened in a basement loft in San Francisco, and it had been revelatory: free of any kind of crazy, any insecurity or games or fraught psychic second-guessing. She was traveling through and we loved each other a little bit for just a little while, a firefly attachment, beautiful and blink it was gone.

But the journal is evidence of someone caught in an undertow. It tells another, darker kind of truth, much of it written through the veil of Scotch at night or the panicked regret of a hangover the next day. I left California and headed back to Texas via Mexico, and though I must have imagined myself some one-woman version of the Wild Bunch, thrilling and free, I was really just colliding with my own troubles on a beach in southern Mexico. I made it to a sleepy little fishing village on the Pacific, with tropical waters and a couple of beach shack restaurants and four-dollar-a-night hotels.

R. had flown to Guadalajara and met me there. What I remember now about those weeks has the layered Photoshop effect of nostalgia: perfect sunsets and midnight swims and the boundless dreams of youth. Memory can be a kind liar. The journal, difficult for me to read, is the scrawl of someone in peril. Someone waffling between adventure and chaotic despair, too young or maybe immature to grasp the sad emptiness of my drama. "This has to change," I wrote. "I'm in southern Mexico and all I'm doing is crying and drinking and taking Librium every day."

A week later, the end of that section: "Sometimes the only thing that seems real to me is what I write."

I got goosebumps when I read the sentence, decades later. So this beat-up black leather diary, filled with bad poetry and clichés, had been my anchor, more than any woman or man had proven to be. At the end of a fight on the beach one night, according to the journal, R. had yelled at me, "You're so unsure of yourself that you can't commit to anything," which I don't remember him saying but now explains a lot. Maybe that was true; I don't know. But within a few months I had left R. and gone back to Austin, and taken up with a woman who I believed, for better or worse, had saved my life.

It's always a crapshoot to give away that kind of power. Maybe some people do it naturally, or more easily than others, or pick wisely, or don't lose themselves in love. I was not that someone, not then. I think now that M. provided me shelter from the storm, a place where I could be safe long enough to regain some stability. And for a time I found that, a sweet spot to land. It didn't last; I spent most of my twenties growing up and out, which may be typical but is difficult to do within the straits of a relationship. But she believed in me, which was a vast gift and more than I was capable of at the time. One night, after too many Scotches or bottles of wine, she stopped me midsentence and said, "Why are you so intellectually downwardly mobile?" Why, in other words, was I so determined to crash and burn?

It shook me up, as though she knew something I couldn't recognize or admit. I was bored and bumming around with dead-end jobs and being a pretend revolutionary, and she had seen through it all and asked the right question. And though we hurt each other terribly—betrayals on both sides, too much booze—and it ended badly, I was always grateful to her for naming my silent enemy that night, which was probably my own fear. And I was strong enough by then to begin to get purchase on my life.

For a while, though, after we broke up, I thought I would die. It felt like an oak tree had been cleaved with an ax. The pain was physical, and sometimes it was hard to breathe, and I treated the pain with whiskey and cigarettes and swam a lot of laps and bored a lot of friends with endless recounts of my saga. What I had discovered, to my idealistic sorrow, was that all the feminism in the world couldn't protect you from psycho-love. By then I was living alone in a peaceful little garage apartment in Austin, and one spring night I was sitting on the porch eating dinner, which included (of course) a bottle of Soave Bolla and fettuccine with green peas. I have a fierce recollection of those peas, that cheap white wine, that view over the trees. I was lonely and sad, but I was finally all right, or knew that I would be. And the evening quiet, just me and the live oaks, felt laden with meaning, as though it were telling me something about the way my story would go.

I went far away, light-years and miles, to escape this period of my life, and for a long time I had nightmares about it—dreams of being in danger and trapped. And I blamed myself, thinking I was hopelessly heterosexual or just made bad choices. I also believed that some of my free fall had to do with relationships between women, who tend to get intimate faster and for whom an emotional connection can turn into a swan dive. But I loved like that twice in my life, once with a woman and years later with a man, once when I was drinking and then when I was sober, and eventually I had to face the notion that what those soul-shredder loves had in common was—me. *Get thee to a therapist,* Hamlet should have said to Ophelia. To hell with nunneries.

I'm older now, and smarter, and my heart no longer looks in the wrong place for the right thing. I've seen the exception too many times to make sweeping statements about gender and love. But I still believe that relationships with women, from my vantage point, have been different in fundamental ways. Women shared a preexisting mutual regard, a tender dignity, that wasn't a foregone conclusion with men. We recognized each other, knew where we'd been. And it wasn't a threat or an ego battle to open up emotionally; it was something we'd always been good for. We had long been the water carriers for the human heart.

I believed this for years, wanted to believe it, even when the data didn't always confirm the hope, or when the lonely crazies could make you think you'd never love or take that risk again. Then I met a writer whose work I admired, who seemed like a southern-made outrageous version of myself, and she made me laugh like I hadn't laughed in a long time. We were like puppies playing together on the beach. I thought, *This is the way it's supposed to feel, happy and free and completely easy.* And it was indeed all those things, for a while. It healed my heart, that romance. To say it didn't last is to somehow suggest that it failed, or we did, when in fact I think the opposite was true—I think we succeeded. We both got precisely what we needed right then, and part of what we needed was a restorative love, without any casualties when it was done.

I can't tell anymore if this is a sad story, desultory periods of love and quiet, love and crazy, finally, different kinds of platonic love, creature love, and solitude. Sometimes it feels frightful, an introvert's life sentence; other nights, eccentric and bold or simply what is. But I suspect it's common to a lot of women who came of age the way I did, under the canopy of the women's movement. We walked away from traditional male-female relationships we couldn't tolerate anymore, acted on options other than marriage and motherhood and toeing the line of the status quo. We made choices that were based utterly on love and strength and want, and the very notion of that freedom felt like a superpower. The fact that some of us wound up alone, for better or worse—that's a by-product of our triumphs. The law of unintended, sometimes poignant, consequences.

I know, too, that everyone's a little broken, and that love's mission, every kind of love, is to reach into the hard places and heal some of the breaks. You learn how to love in spite of the wounds, carry duct tape and prayer and just keep loving.

10

Austin, the late 1970s. I've gone back to graduate school to save my life. I drive a pickup truck, argue with my male professors, have a reputation as an uppity Marxist who will cause trouble in seminars. Being uppity is easy in a department run by several white males from Harvard and Yale, all of them smug with their self-perceptions of liberalism. I am appalled at the competitive, stifling nature of academe, and am also finding out that I am easily as competitive as everyone else.

I am living with a woman, having an affair with a male professor, sick of both romances and champing at the bit to get out of it all—out of Texas, out of love, out of scholarly pursuits. When the time comes to pick a subject for a master's thesis, I unearth a number of women writers from the 1930s, a group called proletarian writers. I write a long, fiery, critically flimsy thesis on these women (Tess Slesinger, Meridel Le Sueur, and Tillie Olsen being the most memorable) and realize (a) how dull it is and (b) that I want to be a working critic, not a campus-bound one.

But first I have to get off the train of higher learning, and I show a draft of the paper to the four members of my committee—all of them men who are rooting for me but also demanding my allegiance. At the end of the day I have crossed campus twice, one office after another, excited and quaking over a range of opinions, and all I can think is how much I need a drink. I am whiplashed from other people's feedback. And then something stops me cold as I stand on that grand, Texas-huge famous forty acres, near the Main Building, near the Tower that Charles Whitman scaled a decade earlier, near the entrance emblazoned with scripture from the book of John: "Ye shall know the truth and the truth shall make you free." When I was a girl of about ten, I saw the building, and the quote gave me goosebumps. Now I'm not just seeking truth, I'm chasing it, hoping for a pat on the head to go along with *veritas*. I've spent months writing about the forgotten voices of women writers, and now I'm desperate for a stamp of approval from four powerful men.

Then I think of something one of the men told me a year or two earlier, the first time we met: "You should get out of here before we ruin you."

And so I do.

11

I t's dark in here, which I will forever think has to do with it being a real psychiatrist's office. I've seen therapists before—both women, friendly, supportive psychologists in Texas who sided with me in the drama of life and sent me on my way. But this is my first M.D., an honest-to-God psychiatrist, which to my thirty-year-old naïve mind means some serious shit, no smiles or Milano cookies like the last one offered. So here we are, in a hospital, even, a famous Boston hospital, nothing funny about it.

She is young, reserved. After I've made a lame effort at being charming, she asks me why I am here. I shrug, slouch in the chair. I am in love with my own sense of tragedy. Everything is fine, really, I say. I just need to figure out how to stop being so self-destructive.

She doesn't flinch, lean forward, give any reaction. She just says, "How many times have you tried?"

At first I am flummoxed, then aghast. She thinks I have attempted suicide. The basic definition of self-destruct. "Oh no!" I say. "I just meant—I'm smoking and drinking myself to death."

Then I remember nothing—not one word, feeling, plan of action—until the end of the hour, after she had told me she wouldn't work with me until I got sober. I do remember saying that I couldn't afford to see her, which was true; I was a freelance writer living on less than $10,000 a year. But I was also relieved that I couldn't afford her, since that pretty much sidelined the notion of my stopping drinking. Which at that point in my life was absolutely, positively, never going to happen. Drinking was my air and water.

I got sober three years later, after the air had become poisoned and it was AA or die. I never saw the woman psychiatrist again, and now, nearly four decades later, I am unsure of her last name or whereabouts. But I've imagined having the chance to thank her, for seeing and saying what I could not. For her gravitas. She must have seen a young woman in trouble, armed with defenses but conflicted enough to have gotten to her office. She heard my flippant words as a cry for help, understood that "self-destructive" had the same final destination in mind, whether slow or fast, conscious or unconscious. It was a long time before I had a glimpse of that correlation. I argued for years that I had never been suicidal, only drunk and desperate and depressed, addicted to any means necessary for escaping reality.

By the time I began the real work of therapy, when I was thirty-eight and five years sober, my therapist had the temerity to suggest that finding alcohol in adolescence may have saved me—might have given me a shield against the depression, a temporary stopgap to grow up enough to save my life. He was a gentle, dry-witted psychiatrist who was the polar opposite of dangerous—of every thrill-seeking attraction that had driven my life. He knew by then of the history of suicide in my family, as well as the alcoholism. I think he glimpsed, too, probably because of my having stopped alcohol, that I had a strong enough superego to keep me from the cliff. I don't know. He trusted me far more than I trusted myself in those years, and while I used to think that simply meant he wasn't yet on to me, now I am flooded with gratitude for his vision and his understanding. Hope, where I had none. Charity, where I knew only self-blame. Steadfastness, above all else. Those eyes of kindness, in the middle of a tornado.

We rebuild the house, the therapist and I. I cry and he stays, I panic and he breathes. The eyes are always on me and he is still, even when I don't get what I want or I descend into rage or despair, the rooms of the past. I read everything I can on this mystical process I have begun, Alice down the rabbit hole of transference. When I stumble onto Alice Miller's *The Drama of the Gifted Child*, I decide to start drawing, because her paintings revealed to her an unconscious she couldn't otherwise reach.

I spend entire winter afternoons drawing, sketches with charcoal and pastels that I find banal and unrevealing. I take them to the therapist and he gasps. I am a critic for a living, but that's in words, not images, so when I draw it's as though my mind has been let out to play. No observing ego here. I draw graveyards, lots of them, and locked fences, and a child crying, and one of a girl in a room, drawing. When the therapist asks me to explain, I say it is the wind blowing through an empty house.

It makes me glad now to remember the pictures, because I did them with such earnest passion—my effort to create a story I didn't know and couldn't tell. I'm still not sure they were all that significant—my adult, critical mind says they were derivative tragic images, some invented icon of sorrow my young subconscious was trying to express. But none of that matters now; blessedly, what I thought about the drawings never mattered. What mattered was that the therapist gasped, and said *Oh my God what have we opened up here?* It was the psychotherapy version of taking a child's sun-and-moon finger painting and giving it prime space on the refrigerator. For a long time he was the sun and I was the moon, and we rebuilt the house so well, I think, that much of our doing so is now a blur.

Everything that mattered over the course of my adult life happened, or re-happened, in that room.

I bring my first Samoyed here when she is nine weeks old. The therapist gives her a small brown bear. She destroys it and I bring home its tattered remains and when she dies thirteen years later I keep it with her ashes.

We have been through a lot of death together, he and I, offstage and on. Vladimir and Estragon, reporting in from the front. Nothing scares him. Wearies, maybe. Never scares.

The therapist loves me. I know this, though he is not allowed to say so. He has been a magisterial choreographer of boundaries over the years. A man on a wire. He has pitched and swayed and held on in the high winds of attachment and terror and awful grief, and still we never plunge from our perch.

He has shown me how to give up anger, a toxic substance I didn't know I craved until I tried to go without it. He never told me to do this, or even suggested it. Instead he showed me what power looked like. It was the force of love, of radical authenticity. No victims were involved.

The therapist's beloved wife dies. I cry until I think my heart will break. I cry like a child, as though someone has thrown a stone at the magic house in the forest, which was supposed to stay protected. I cannot bear that he must bear this pain.

I keep the drawings for years and years, and then one day I unceremoniously throw them away. Nothing was lost. I drew, he responded. Cast out the net. My message in a bottle.

I tend to remember arduous efforts more than triumphs. Maybe it's because the triumphs seem easy in retrospect, when one is standing on the hill at the end of the ascent. The climb takes longer, is more telling: being cold or alone, wanting to give up, getting to your feet and staggering forth. The rest is gravy.

Then a friend reminds me that Tyler would not leave out her triumphs. She's right: Tyler's stories—knights on flying horses, a broken leg that mends overnight to win a race—are always victories. So here's one of mine.

April 2001. On a Friday afternoon in early spring, I find out from my editor at the *Globe* that I have won the Pulitzer Prize. The prizes will be announced on Monday, and I am sworn to secrecy until then. Within hours I will break this vow by calling my best friend, Caroline, who is out of town until Sunday, and my eighty-six-year-old mother, who is in Texas. But for now the news is mine, a mind-blowing, humbling piece of news.

I am completely adither, so I go for a row on the Charles River. The river is empty: cold, cloudy, nobody out at midday. I row along in a mild stupor, grateful for this moment of suspended time.

Each October, the boathouse that I row out of hosts the Head of the Charles Regatta. What the Boston or New York Marathon is to runners, the Head of the Charles is to rowers. I know the three-mile course, know where the understated concrete post is that marks the finish line. The post is like a tiny Stonehenge to racers, many of whom are world-class athletes. I thrill to watch it every autumn, but I lack the skill ever to row in the Head; I'm too slow, too small.

Today, though, with no one around, I row part of the course. I turn around and angle my boat in the right direction when I'm nearing the final stretch, and in the last twenty yards I manage a rare set of masterful strokes. I cross the finish line on an empty river and throw up one hand, mime a victory cheer.

One of the reasons I love this memory is that it happened when Caroline was still alive. She was the only person I ever told about it. A year later, almost to the day, we would find out she had stage four lung cancer; seven weeks after that, she was gone. She was forty-two. But during that spring of 2001, we were both still rowing, still laughing about how someday we would row the Head together. We thought we had all the world and time.

ONE SUMMER AFTERNOON TYLER CONVINCES ME TO let her train me as an entry-level genie. Tula is snoring in the foyer; it is too hot for a walk and too early to swim. Why not study genie-ism? Soon I am sitting on the couch in the lotus position, eyes closed, and she elbows me if I open them. For homework, apparently, I must read the *Odyssey*—a book Tyler picked at random off a living room shelf, probably because it looked ponderously long. She has laid down a few critical rules of the training: "Number one: You must never use your magic for evil purposes. Number two: You have three wishes, and you can always wish for more wishes. And number three: You are not allowed to wish for a nap." (I suspect another inductee got sleepy during training.)

We are knee-to-knee on the sofa, as quiet as we have ever been. I drift into a happy, dreamy space. After a while Tyler's dramatically deep voice says, "You may now open your eyes."

When I look at her, she is right up next to me, her eyelids fluttering, her body still as stone. In a kind of *Exorcist*-but-not-scary voice she says, "My name is

Sunshine and I am a thousand years old. You can find me anywhere and I will come to you. You may even come to me while I am sleeping and I will find you."

I break position and put my arm around her. Nobody need worry about this child's sense of self. She feels tethered to the entire universe.

12

When I was hired as a book critic by *The Boston Globe* in 1985, I did a first round of interviews with seven editors. One of the questions I got was about working for a big-city daily. The *Globe* had a readership large enough to freeze my hands before the keyboard when I thought about it. My background was in academia, and as a freelancer for alternative weeklies, where I usually had several days or weeks to finish a story. Would I be able to keep up with the time imperatives of writing on deadline, file from the field if necessary?

I swallowed and said yes, absolutely, but it was a bluff of confidence. I'd never written so fast for so many. A year later, when the PEN writers' congress convened in New York for a week, I flew on winged feet to cover it. I was thirty-four, and roaming the lobby of a midtown hotel with the likes of Toni Morrison, Günter Grass, Grace Paley, Salman Rushdie. The place was lousy with famous writers. There hadn't been anything like it in fifty years, since the writers' congresses of the 1930s, and I was determined to do it justice.

I filed every day, sometimes twice when there was real news, like the protests that Norman Mailer led over the appearance of then–secretary of state George Shultz. I wrote my stories in longhand and dictated them from a phone booth to a night editor and felt like Lois Lane. The last night of the convention, I went to a nearby well-known steakhouse and asked the waiter for advice. He looked askance when I mentioned a particular piece of meat, and I ordered it anyway, assuming he was treating me like an out-of-town rube.

Always trust a side-eye from a waiter. I woke up heaving at three A.M., the start of a case of food poisoning that still humbles me to remember it. For hours I was too sick to move, but there was a closing keynote address by Mario Vargas Llosa at ten A.M., and I needed it on tape; then I could write the final story from Boston. Somehow I made it downstairs and found rice pudding and tea at the corner deli, and got inside the main ballroom. The last thing I remember is holding my tape recorder high in the air.

When I came to I was on the floor in the women's lounge, surrounded by New York City firefighters and a kind woman who had been standing next to me in the ballroom and had seen me go down. She said I looked green before I fainted. I explained about the food poisoning. I must have already been packed to leave, because someone got me and my suitcase to the office of the midtown doctor on call for the hotel.

I can still see the glaring sunlight coming through the windows of his examining room, the nurse disappearing with a frown on her face. And I can hear the slimy tone in the doctor's voice as he leaned close to my face. I was so ill, so dehydrated, and yet there was no mystery about what was wrong with me—I had told the firemen and the people at the hotel and this nurse that I had food poisoning, had eaten a bad steak.

The doctor speaks softly in my ear. "I can give you a shot of Compazine that will make you feel better. Would you like that?" The voice is silky, creepy, as though he has the magic potion but I must dance for it. I know about Compazine, a powerful (and sedating) antiemetic that stops nausea on a dime, and I nod through my groans. Then his voice is coming from the end of the table, where he is standing between my knees. "Now I need to do a full pelvic exam."

I drift off. There is the voice again, near my head, a

hand on my waist. "You can sleep in here. The nurse is leaving soon and you can stay here as long as you like."

I come to scrambling, clawing my way awake, thinking *I have to get out of here.* I am so weak I can barely walk. I get dressed lying down, grab my bag, stagger out toward that too-bright sunlight. The waiting room is empty and the doctor calls out, half-plaintively. I keep going. Wonder of wonders, I get a cab in ten seconds and make it to LaGuardia.

A close friend in Boston is an ob/gyn. When I tell her the story a few days later, her brow furrows. I watch her face and see her decide to display calm rather than distress. "I suppose you could make a case that he had to check for a perforated bowel," she says, wanting to console me. "But that would really be a stretch."

I get a bill from the doctor's office. I could easily add it to my expense account, where it would be taken care of. Instead I throw it away. I never hear from the doctor again.

———

We are walking on a deserted beach, the Famous Writer and I. I've pursued him for an interview, traveled to his summer home to find him, and after a day of talking we discover that we both love dogs and walking and swimming. I know a place, he tells me, we'll go there tomorrow. We pile in the car with his two sweet retrievers, and because I'm staying at a B&B and unequipped, he assures me he has towels for the dogs and for us.

The swim is a good one: brisk late-summer waters under a cloudless sky. I'm always outfitted for a swim, whenever I travel: two black racing suits for ocean or pond water, cap and goggles and spares of each. We both swim far out, away from each other, and after half an hour or so I walk in to the shore. He has a bath towel waiting for me and spreads it on the ground so that I can sit.

Then I realize there is just the one towel.

He sets his two-hundred-pound, twenty-years-older body next to me, about four inches away, and smiles companionably and looks out to sea. We are on a keyed beach, accessible only to the gilded few. "You know there's no one around for miles," Famous Writer tells me, his eyes straight ahead. "We could be here for another hour and never see a soul." Then he moves a little closer.

I spent months trying to get this interview. I've gone around his publisher, jumped the gun on a radio silence he agreed to with his agent, gotten access no other paper will have for several weeks. We've sat for hours in the afternoon shade of his study, talking about families and despair and art and drinking and how to build a day or a life that's worth keeping. I will go back to Boston and write my story, my big triumphant scoop of a story. But not before FW makes a self-congratulatory, quasi-chivalrous pass at me.

We sit there in silence and I am slightly embarrassed for him. I cough out something like "It's really beautiful here" and then get up abruptly. "I'm going in again," I say, and wade back into the ocean. Ten minutes later the moment is over. He has taken the hint and shrugged it off, his ego untouched, as though he just wanted me to know that he was available for a quickie on the beach, while his wife prepared our lunch back at the house.

I tell no one about this encounter because I like FW and I think it's unseemly and puts him in a bad light. More important to me are his wife and children, whom I would not want to hurt or embarrass. When after weeks I confide to a friend what happened, someone who knows him and who I believe will be discreet, she tells me, to my horror, that she thinks I should be flattered.

After my story appears, I listen with a mask of composure if people comment on the depth of the interview. I have left out the towel, the one moment when he fell from grace and then recovered, because I respect him and, seriously, such things happen to women journalists all the time. I too shrug it off. For the year after the story appears he stays in contact occasionally, writing several times from another state and making similarly polite, one-towel offers. "I could drive up and we could go for a ride." That sort of thing. I demur, decline, plead a busy schedule. Always polite.

Decades later this still pisses me off, partly at myself. Because, as usual, the woman winds up protecting the man, the one who crossed a line, insulted me, acted like a patronizing literary giant trying to get a little on the side. Up until today, I thought I'd never write this story, because who would be helped, why does it matter? The usual inner narrative where I swallow and look away.

And then I realized what I wish I had said, what I might not have known to say then, as my fortysomething self, and so I can say it now.

I wish I had sat on that towel and not moved an inch, and stayed looking out to sea, like he did. And said quietly, "You know, you probably don't realize it, but I'm the one with all the power here.

"Sure, you're the renowned writer who's making a pass and trying to do it politely. And I'm just a tyro who's pursued you, hungry for copy, fawning and asking all the right questions, talking about you and your work for hours.

"But here's the thing: I work for a newspaper with a circulation of more than a million, and my story isn't written yet. It could go either way."

Then I might have gotten up, patted the dogs, and said, "Great swim. Should we go have some lunch?"

13

I saw a coyote this morning at the cemetery, his tawny profile only a few yards away. It happened fast, and the dog didn't even seem surprised. Her nose tells her far more than I can comprehend about who's been here ahead of us. We all three froze: the coyote, insouciant and wild, went still in protective camouflage; the dog, bigger by ten pounds, watched and waited. And I, the apex predator, just froze in order to grab the image, etch it onto memory. It was the nearest I'd ever been to a coyote. Then the moment broke and I called the dog and clattered a stick on a tree, loudly. And off he went.

Tyler will be thrilled: She is in love with all things wild right now. I've seen coyote only once before on these grounds, though I have spotted a red fox, groundhog, chipmunk, vole, and a rabbit who had just given birth in an open field and wouldn't leave her nest. When I realized how exposed the rabbit was I ran at her and clapped my hands, hoping to get her out of harm's way. But she moved only long enough for me to see what she was shielding—a litter of newborn kits, still in their amniotic sac. I gasped and retreated and she returned to her post. Maternal instinct had won out over fear. I doubt the litter survived the night.

I've been walking this cemetery for years, by now a pilgrim's trek that began as a dilettante's stroll. I just came here one day to walk the dog. But it was the winter after my father died, buried in Texas, and two years after I'd lost my best friend, buried nowhere, and I see now that I needed a place to go—a place to find what was missing. I used to lean up against the fence in the corner of the veterans field and talk to my mom, too, gone more than a decade now, and to this day I imagine stories that go with the names and dates on the soldiers' markers.

The place is a cathedral of meaning, much of it unfolding in the tributes left by the living. One year, a pair of black patent high heels shows up on the headstone of a long-married couple. Birthday balloons and playing cards, a box of Milk Duds. At two graves I visit, I leave small rocks on the headstones—my wave from this side of the river. The graves belong to people who died more than a century ago, and stay bare from year to year. But I've grown a filament of care for them over time, so I leave the rocks.

I've always felt at ease in cemeteries, where the veil lifts long enough to cinch my heart to what I've lost. Grief is worse untethered, I think, when it doesn't have a home. And this is a universe entire of people gone and people missed; here on the great beach of time, my losses soften and recede. There are other regulars I see from afar—bird-watchers, a sketch artist who once asked for directions. One man who walks the same route every day, the opposite direction from me, and we nod and smile. I think of him as The Walker, though that is probably how he thinks of me as well. People are mostly silent here, not discounting the woman who sits near her husband's grave with a lawn chair, talking.

Veterans from three major wars lie here, and old New England families, and people who died too young. Whenever the Patriots or the Red Sox take a big win, the fields light up with sports caps and pennants, a New England version of Día de los Muertos. Some days everything about the place feels sacred: You can hear kids' voices from the athletic field that abuts the cemetery, the megaphone shout from a crew coach on the nearby Charles. It's an intersection of the messy ongoing fact of life and the stillness of its end. No unfinished arguments here, no power plays or murderous impulses, not anymore. The wolf finally did lie down with the lamb.

The past couple of years have been so brutal. So much change, so many injuries revealed, public and private. The meanness of the world exposed. I need this place, this quiet dust. My solace for an hour or so each day, even if confined to memory and myth.

14

Honey, don't do that. It's unbecoming." Maybe I had sworn, though more likely I'd crossed my leg ankle-over-knee, like my dad did, or slouched or rolled my eyes. "Unbecoming" was my mother's admonishment of choice—at least until I became much worse than that—and her correction rolled off the tongue with casual ease. It was her code for what she might have called "class," also achieved by walking with a book on your head (good posture) or keeping your knees together (good girl) or the common jingle for pec isometrics ("We must! We must! We must improve the bust!").

My mother was never harsh when she labeled a behavior unbecoming. She was trying to pass on what she knew, and with me she had her work cut out for her.

For a teenage girl in the Texas Panhandle in the early 1960s, there were so many obstacles to clear: miniskirts, dark lipstick, splayed legs, smoking, cursing, Everclear parties, back seats with boys. As I got older and farther away from the nest, the challenges got grander and the dares more dangerous. Drugs, hitchhiking, wild men, wild women, protests of every magnitude. A whole landscape—a life—of things unbecoming. First innocent, then eager, I tried them all.

The origin of the usage of "unbecoming" is military, and suggests an order broken, a fall from civilized behavior not befitting, say, an officer and a gentleman. By the time the word fell into the vernacular to describe female behavior, it had taken on a cautionary aura: "Unbecoming," at least when my mother and the women of her generation said it, sounded just this side of slatternly. The word hinted at something shameful, and the accent that delivered it, at least in my memory, was a testament of southern refinement. *That's so unbecoming.* Annihilation by etiquette. Crushed by a crystal dinner bell.

Certainly there was no crystal dinner bell in our house, or in my mother's—her mother, a Texas farmer's wife who wore jeans and laughed loudly, rang a large brass dinner bell on the back porch when she hollered to announce a meal. So "unbecoming" had a little class aspiration to it, too: Its manifest opposite was "becoming," heading up a staircase in the clouds toward a better life.

Two of my aunts had direct and radical paths to unbecoming. "We found Billie on the bathroom floor this morning," my grandmother wrote, describing one of several of Billie's efforts to no longer be. It was sleeping pills that time, and years later, when she died, they simply wrote "heart failure" on the death certificate. Sometimes medical euphemism is the only bearable salve for tragedy. I didn't get that then. When I learned, far after the fact, about the troubles in my extended family, I was indignant that I hadn't been told before. I was old enough to challenge family myths but too selfish or green to understand them. You have to have your heart smashed to comprehend why people mess with the narrative in order to live.

Aunt Connie's dissolution took longer, its path punctuated by shock treatments, hospitalizations, bad marriages, disappearing into the bottle. I look like her, my mother used to tell me, and I was pleased by the comparison: She was a high school basketball star and swimmer, all legs and smiles before the bad stuff began, and to me she was the epitome of an independent, mysterious woman. She loved dogs and reading and fishing with my dad, and she let me hide out in her room and read her novels when we were at the family farm. I adored her and was slightly scared of her, and she died suddenly, around fifty, when I was fifteen. It must have been my first real taste of grief, the leaden feeling, and I can almost see the air that day, it hung so heavy at the gravesite. I remember the dress I wore and the way the trees looked out the car window as we drove home from Breckenridge, where she was buried. I was so sad, sad in a whole new way. I was facing a despondency about something that I knew wouldn't change. That dead was dead. All the things you think are obvious truths until you feel them like a stone upon your heart.

Are all teenaged girls drawn to tragedy? It was a touchstone of my adolescence: the bad poems I wrote with funereal images, the anthologies dog-eared at Plath and Dickinson and Sexton. In the margin of Dickinson's "Pain has an element of blank," in *Norton*'s third, there are four slashed stars in ink, as though I had just discovered (and I had) a terse, holy definition of the fugue of despair. At first I hid this side of me; later, I made a lame effort to cultivate a persona around it. My mother saw the books and read a few of the poems and her inevitable comment was "Don't *brood*"—as though such sadness might be turned off like a leaky tap.

She must have worried that what she glimpsed in me was too close to what she had seen in her sisters. But brood away I did, even happily, finding respite in heroines whose troubles trumped my own. I clung to these stories through my young adulthood, through my years in academe, and then I started to see the strings of the puppet master behind the tragedy. Tolstoy sending Anna K. to her death. Hardy giving his Tess a lethal mix of lust and innocence that made her downfall all but certain. Everywhere I looked there was some guy creating a tragic heroine and then tying her to the railroad tracks. If women authors could be just as murderous, their intentions seemed to reflect a different kind of suffering—less distant, less cold, and less titillating. Maybe that's why I loved Faulkner so much and so early—he sent Quentin off a bridge but let us keep his beloved Caddy.

I stumbled upon these insights on my own, which was fortunate for me—if I'd been taught them in the new critical theory invading the campuses in the seventies, I think I'd have lost what moxie I possessed. I fled those theorists, whose ideas for me diced and deconstructed novels into shards of eye-glazing dullness. What I had instead was a cache of half-interpreted novels behind me, most of them read on the sly, and the cultural heft of a women's movement that made me trust my own opinion. That combination, free of cant, was what gave me the courage to throw a typewriter in the back of my old Volvo and decide that I could be a writer. Or that I would never forgive myself if I didn't try.

Nearly four decades later, I remember that journey—the geographic one out of Texas and the interior one toward a calling—as dangerous but worth the risk, unlike so many of the treks I made over unsafe terrain. This one had an end in mind, a plan and a self worth saving, even if I did have to go mano a mano with Scotch in an attic apartment. I had my mecca in sight.

I had almost fallen, though, for an old trope: that high bridge between death and liberation, a gratifyingly tragic ending that we embrace in modern culture without a second thought. It's the Thelma-and-Louise promise of going out strong, but its origins are ancient. Now I see it as a cheap ploy, a fantasy about sacrifice and art or heroism, but the myth is intractable. It's a warrior-martyr mentality, and the allure is different for women, a blood sport of self-destruction. In the past half century we've gone from hiding anguish to fetishizing it. Some of the early feminist icons appropriated their pain as an act of reclamation, then left themselves on the marble slab of art. "The woman is perfected. / Her dead / Body wears the smile of accomplishment," wrote Plath in "Edge," in *Ariel.* And then Anne Sexton's near-retort, upon hearing of Plath's suicide, ". . . I know at the news of your death, / a terrible taste for.it, like salt."

Why did happy and free always have to be so far apart?

15

J ohn and I both declared we wanted to learn the cello when we got old. "When I get old . . ."—that territory, the color of clouds, that tethers the present by promising a future. We sat in newsrooms together for more than two decades, and on nights we had to wait for page proofs, we let our tired minds wander. The cello suited us both, expressing the dark sensibility we shared but rarely discussed. Instead we matched each other for shots of Stolichnaya in the bar across the street, or swapped passages of novels we loved. We complained about mediocre writing; when one of us made a comment about the dilution of modern litera-ture, John started a list of watered-down titles as a joke and hung it in the newsroom: Stendhal's *The Pink and the Gray*, Dostoyevsky's *Misdemeanors and Time-Outs*,

Faulkner's *The Noise and the Kerfuffle*. By the end of the day, thanks to the shared wit of the staff, it was two pages long.

Humor and intellect masked his pain: A former coworker wrote about John that he was so confident he didn't own a dictionary, nor did he need one. The story was apocryphal, but then John's editorial skill merited the inflation. To disappoint him was an awful feeling, though he responded with gentle civility. But to please him was a great joy. Once I wrote a headline he admired and he walked into my office and bowed, like a knight to his queen. Only because he knew so much more than the rest of us did we swoon in the face of such praise.

John didn't grow old. Instead, at fifty-two, he left the house for work, his reading glasses in his pocket, and climbed into his Volvo station wagon. He started the engine but didn't raise the garage door. Upstairs he had left letters for his wife and daughters. The rest of us—all of us—were left with that cavern of doubt and speculation that is the one-way dialogue after a suicide.

You can always tell the story but that's never enough. It explains nothing, or rather explains a mere glimpse of the chasm that is suicidal depression, gives you a snapshot of a particularly bad day with the most fixed of endings. We are always frantic for a reason: a bad diagnosis, a drug problem, an unhappy home life. Please, God, name a reason so I can protect myself from the contagion that is life, the horrifying notion that someone I knew or loved or admired chose to leave because . . . the dark at that moment eclipsed the light.

The service was devastating. I was one of the people from John's work life who were speaking, and I labored over my remarks for days. On the way to the church I had to pull the car over and breathe. I didn't drink anymore and I didn't smoke and I couldn't call my friend Caroline, who had died two years earlier, so I sat there and watched my hands shake and then closed my eyes.

When I got into the pew where the other speakers were sitting, I saw that they looked how I felt. How do you say goodbye to someone who chose the early exit? What can you say that is true and honoring and most of all a consolation? Only one of us dared to hit it head-on, and she turned to John's daughters and looked at them as she spoke. "The depression that *took* John was not John," she said, with such tenderness and enunciation that she clarified a truth that often goes unspoken. Suicidal depression is an interloper who breaks into your house. It is not the man himself, the father who laughed with you and went apple picking and edited clumsy young writers hours past their dead-line. It's a stranger, a condition that won the fight that day. The depression is the perpetrator.

Tell me about my dad. His older daughter asked me this and I wanted to weep, and I said that yes, of course, I would. I never did. I never could. I knew she wanted to know everything, she wanted to fill her pockets with stories she hadn't heard and days when she hadn't been there; she wanted a father to keep.

One thing I didn't tell her, and ought to have, is that John's soft voice kept me sane when my own father died—when I was on my way home to Texas to bury him. I had fled town when my mother called to say that my father was failing, and I'd left a review that was run-ning that week, and John stepped in to take over. He called while I was in flight and left a message on my cellphone, telling me not to worry, that he had taken care of everything. And then he said a few things about losing my father that were so kind and true that I played the message, again and again, as I walked, tears on my face, through the airport terminal.

I tried to talk to him once about his drinking, years after I had gotten sober, when I knew it had him by the throat. He blew me off, appreciative but distant. The week before he died, in 2004, I handed in the manu-script for my first book, and out of nowhere the thought crossed my mind that I couldn't possibly send in some-thing so naked, something that John hadn't edited. Everything I'd written for years had passed through his hands. A week later I got the call, at nine P.M., that he had died, and I threw the phone across the room.

I was only a bit player in his life. Not a wife, a daughter, a sister, a close friend. Suicide's concentric circles cannot be imagined, I think, by the person at the end of that long hallway, who in his final reasoning has found a way to believe that he is doing the best thing for everyone. And yet each step leaves the notion of "every-one" further and further behind.

Five men I've known well have chosen suicide, or rather suicide chose them; only one woman. Women try in far greater numbers, but men succeed, at least in the United States, by almost four to one. This is known as the gender paradox in the epidemiology of suicide, with one speculation being that men choose more direct or violent means: a rope, a cliff, a gun. Less quan-tifiable is the notion that women are more likely to reach out, get help. Every demographic has its guiding detail: weather, cultural or sociological status, the effects of war. The reasons are always particular and univer-sal, a mystery and a fact that can't be undone.

I heard a story about a musical prodigy who ended his life because, his friends believed, he could not bear the internal pressure of trying to live up to his talent, which he had come to loathe. His gift had become a scourge. The story broke my heart. An envy to the outside world may be a private prison. A woman came into an AA meeting one night and broke down, sobbing over her failed efforts to get clean. She had tried again and again to no avail. Choking, she said, "The thing is, I want to live." Those last four words: the most important ones, a vessel of hope. I want to think she made it.

When my mother was in her late seventies and I was years sober, when the fear and trouble between us was in the far past, she confessed how worried she had been during my adolescence. "I was scared," she told me. "I was afraid that you would take your life."

The thing is, Mom, I never would have. Never. Even on the worst days, there was too much here. Even when I was drunk and heartsick in that attic apartment, my first year in the Northeast—when I was estranged from everything I knew and cared about. Except for the idea that I might become a writer.

And I guess that's what it comes down to, for everybody. You have to find something you love enough in this world to stay in it.

16

Caroline and I were walking in the woods, a setting that might have defined half our physical time together in the seven years we had. We loved the woods outside of Boston, the trails near Franconia Notch in New Hampshire, the marshes on the Vineyard and the pond paths near Truro. Cat Rock, Mount Misery, Wellfleet's Great Island Trail. We weren't picky, so long as we had the dogs and each other and some water and maybe chocolate and a car to get us home.

I remember this day in particular, though, and I don't know why. I can see the sun falling through leaves and I can feel that it is autumn—the temperature cool—and I know, too, that I was in a familiar zone of discontent, a feeling I made worse by berating myself. Caroline, more than anyone I'd ever known, recognized the dark place I could catapult into, and she knew how to convince me it was an illusion.

One of the ways she did so was by telling me a story, *my* story, as though I were five or had never heard it before. She cleared her throat, used her hands to make the point. "May I remind you," she said. "You moved to Boston." She blocked out each sentence with her hands, as though every life event deserved, say, a running foot. "You got sober. You started work at the *Globe*. You started therapy. You got Clementine" (my first Samoyed). Here she gave me the side-eye and smiled. "And me, I might add."

Yes, you, I might add, twenty-plus years later.

I grabbed on to every memory I had after she died. Like a desperate shopper in one of those giveaway races against the clock, throwing everything within reach into the cart. I could almost feel my brain whirring in the first weeks after she was gone, etching into history every laugh, eye roll, physical gesture. The day she steadied me on our first walk, when I tripped on a root in the path. The ropy muscles of those forearms, the arms that rowed the Charles and swam the ponds and that I held on to for hours in the last weeks of her life.

I've written about her before, but you don't forget people when they die; you don't stop loving them or relying on them. I know we can romanticize the dead. I try not to do it. She's been gone a long time now and I think about how it might be if she were here, if we had had the friendship we thought would go on for decades. It's a heartbreaking game because the rules are mutable and time always wins and there's no alternate reality where I didn't change and she didn't die.

So. The rule, the platitude, is that you have to go on. Which we do, most of us, some more creatively and easily than others. I survived Caroline's death, and losing her shaped my life, because a loss like that—it's like the heart is returning from war; it is simply never the same. And everything good we had—the depth of the friendship, the trust, the laughter—those were the things I got to keep. The force that allowed me to stick around, mow the grass, love and lose dogs, bury my parents, grow old, love new people. I miss her still.

Nearly a decade after Caroline died I went back to Austin, where I was reading at a book festival, and where half the women I'd come of age with still lived. Someone threw a party, and one of my friends toasted me because I was home, and we all started talking about the old days, as well as the book I'd written about Caroline and the different losses all of us had been through. I looked around the room at those beautiful, aging faces I'd known for so many years and saw something I'd not known before. "You guys," I said. "I never could have had the friendship I did with Caroline without all of you. You—everything we all went through—is what taught me how to be that close, be that kind of friend."

If the emotional legacies of the women's movement blessed our friendship, so did living in a post–Title IX world. She taught me to row and I taught her to swim; we spent hours together in the water or on it, or walking and talking about it. The intense physicality of our experience made it wider and more intimate at once, a largesse I would miss like a phantom limb when she was gone. By the time Caroline and I became friends, in the 1990s, women's athletic prowess was a societal given. But females had a far more limited range of expressing intimacy when I was growing up. They had shopping and makeup and competing over boys, unless you also throw in home economics, a mandatory class I came close to flunking after nearly setting the cooking lab on fire. In postwar America, the window had closed on the women's athletics that were a part of the 1930s; by my high school years, just as rock and roll was blowing open the culture, girls had few sanctioned ways to express a love of the natural world and their own bodies in it. I became a swimmer as a young girl because I'd had polio and was less stable on land than in water, not because female athletics were encouraged. They didn't even exist, not in the Panhandle in the 1950s or '60s.

I saw a young runner one day at the nearby reservoir, where she was mostly likely training for the Boston Marathon. She was doing three-mile circuits, passing me every several minutes for another lap, and I commented to a friend how beautiful she looked—all that grace and power. "We didn't really have that," Shannon said, matter-of-factly, and I was so startled by this notion that I came home and dug out my high school annual, class of 1968. Sports in the Panhandle of Texas. Seven pages were devoted to football. Boys had eight or nine sports—wrestling, track and field, baseball, football, tennis, golf, basketball—which ran on for seventeen pages. Girls had two: cheerleading and gym. There's a photo of gym class, with three or four awkward girls in white cotton uniforms, standing around in eye makeup with their arms crossed. A snapshot of history, ludicrous and painful, and revealing for what isn't there. The missing pages.

Some of this was a matter of geography and privilege as well as gender: The Ivies tended to train the girls in all kinds of ways that were not in the Texas rule book. Texas girls could triumph in barrel racing, but that took money (and a horse). What we didn't have was some avenue, some way to feel our own life force growing up and through space. You don't much think about what you haven't yet learned, what you didn't have a chance at, and I marvel a little at the irony of what this absence created in me—the polio that slowed me down on land gave me the water instead.

My love for Caroline was a defining relationship in my life, and it coincided with a time when I was beginning to feel the strength and freedom of a certain age. For me this was my early forties: You're old enough to be street-smart and young enough to run a marathon. I had work that I loved as a book critic and I was raising my first Samoyed, a beautiful fifty-plus-pound sled dog who enhanced everything already good about my days. I had weekly deadlines, and the pool and the woods and a woman friend who might have been my twin, but for the fact that she already had a twin. A few years earlier I had left a man I loved, or thought I had loved, but in fact was held hostage by, desperate as I was for his praise and his love. He was the last chapter in a rough decade, years sometimes colored by a crummy romantic relationship. An obsession, a heartbreak, a tragic narrative. My work and my sobriety were what saved me. And my friendships with women, particularly Caroline. I think we each grew into our reflections; we grew into the person that the other one already saw standing there. We loved in one another the strengths we didn't know we had alone.

The man whose praise I was desperate for often read and edited what I wrote before it saw print. A turning point came for me in one of these blue-pencil moments. I had managed to get a rare interview with John le Carré, and I was pleased with the way I'd begun the story. (If time is any indicator of certainty, thirty years later, I still am.) I watched as he read, his brow furrowed. I saw him pause and then cross out my first sentence. "Too flashy," he said.

The pause was what gave him away. It was a look I'd seen a couple of times before, in graduate school and in the writing world, when a man I had respected flinched and tried to put me in my place. I was eleven years younger here, and the better writer, and I knew it.

Once he was through editing, I thanked him and took the copy into my study. I restored my words to the way I'd written them. The story ran two days later, on the section front. He read it over breakfast, and raised his eyebrows and looked at me. I smiled.

. . .

The week of the Christine Blasey Ford testimony and Brett Kavanaugh hearings, and we are in yet another time warp. Pandora's box has been opened with a crowbar over the past two years, hope lingering inside, the evils that women held on to as secrets spilling out like crazy. I am talking to a friend (as is every other woman I know) about our own sexual histories, about speaking truth to power. About what to do when truth whispers or yells and power doesn't really care. I say I feel lucky that no sexual assault, micro or macro, took me down. Or left irreparable damage, messed me up in ways known or unknown. I don't consider this anything more than dumb luck. People keep and contain and release trauma in myriad ways.

Then my friend reminds me of something. "You got your father's strength," she says, even though she never knew my father but has known me many years. "It's almost as if you breathed it in."

And credit where it's also due: My mother took guff from no man. I saw her stand up to men with more power and money and education than she ever dreamed of, men she even feared, but in the end they got out of her way or held the door. She stood less than five three and was afraid of almost nothing, which is why I'd pick her for my team every time.

We're all wearied from the stories. Too many assaults, major and minor, too many revelations and confessions and oh-my-God remembrances. So I've been selective in the ones I've told. Here's what I left out: The *New York Times* editor who insisted on buying me dinner, then started stroking my bare upper arm as he told me he didn't have a job to offer me—yet. The men writers I interviewed who lunged at me after they'd had a drink or two. I left out the colleagues and other women's husbands who have grabbed me inappropriately. The professors. The flashers on the river and in the woods, the creeps on the sidewalk at ten P.M., the catcalls and presumptions of everyday life. And hey, nothing special going on here. If I'd been a welder or lived on a ranch all my life or served in the military, I'd have different stories with a similar bent. They're as common as bad traffic or the flu.

THE OLDER TYLER GETS, THE MORE SHE WANTS AN update on the old-boyfriend or -girlfriend story, even though I remind her often that if you don't marry, life is long and so is the list of exes. But she persists: Just *tell* me. So I begin again with early boyfriends, high school breakups, summer romances. She wants the whole parade and I edit wildly as I go, knowing one story is too boring, one too inconsequential. Then suddenly I find myself in the swamp of young adulthood that for me included drugs, long-haired boys, an arrest here and there. I realize the story is changing and so I stop.

Do you know about drugs? I ask. This precocious child looks confused, and I realize she thinks I mean things like penicillin and milk of magnesia. Oh, you mean marijuana! she says. Yes, I say, and then I get emphatic. "You have to promise me something, OK?" She nods, slightly alarmed at how serious I've become.

"You have to promise that if, years from now or whenever, you decide to try alcohol and drugs, you'll come talk to me first." She shushes me and says OK OK OK.

"But, Gail," she says. "I don't need to try drugs." She shows me her palms, as though all this is obvious. "I'm already awesome."

One day when Tyler is in the middle of a long story, she interrupts herself and says, as if it just occurred to her, "If you live alone there's no one to talk to!" But mostly she seems to think I've gotten away with something. The first time she saw me drink milk straight from the carton, her eyes widened. "I could *never* do that at my house!" "Of course you couldn't," I say, "this is what you get to do if you live alone. Plus you can have ice cream in the middle of the night, with chunks of broken cookies, and walk the dog at midnight, and no one ever tells you what time to go to bed."

Even without my editorial, she is fascinated by the freedoms: a TV in the kitchen, swims on winter evenings, dinner on the couch. "If you got married now, you'd be in the *Guinness Book of World Records*!" she says. We both laugh. In her mind I am living life as a giant child, or a wrinkled teenager, or some perfect mix of freedom and pleasure. A semi-myth I do little to dissuade.

17

And now Marjorie must make an appearance on this stage. A white-haired, valiant woman who lived by no rule book and thus wrote one, unknowingly, for all the younger women who adored her. I didn't know her when she was a knockout, but rather decades later, when she had become what knockouts age into if they are lucky: confident and uncaring, her laughter like an aria, her stride outpacing even the border collie—she had five over the years—who was always by her side. Cory was the last of them, a tricolor who walked next to her off-lead all over Cambridge, staring adoringly as she spoke to him in full paragraphs. Marjorie had been in England with her mother in her late thirties, and they had gone to the lake country to watch the legendary sheepdogs at herding trials. She came home straightaway, as she put it, located a breeder of a working line, and began an extraordinary arc of human-dog relationships that spanned the next forty years.

But then most of Marjorie's relationships seemed extraordinary, at least as viewed from the outside, or by the other person in them. When I met her she had just retired from decades of teaching at Shady Hill, a progressive private school in Cambridge, where she influenced a generation of students and teachers both. "She changed my life," people kept saying at the memorial a few months after she died. She was born to privilege in Scarsdale, New York, in 1932, and became an economics major and field hockey star at Swarthmore—this when girls didn't necessarily go to college, much less storm the field or pretend to understand money, its curves and mystery and unpredictability. Those traits belonged instead to femininity in the fifties, which wasn't of much interest to Marjorie. She was a little embarrassed by her background, and the doorways it opened were of no interest to her unless the path could help someone else. After college she got involved in the burgeoning civil rights movement, teaching in the inner-city schools in Chicago until she came to Cambridge.

It's a classic tale, the liberal bluestocking from an

elite station wading into the social justice causes of the 1960s. I have a hunch that Marjorie was a red from the first time she encountered private property, probably in the sandbox. She possessed some elemental sense of fairness, evident from the moment you met her. Because of her physical prowess, you could recognize from a block away the alacrity with which she moved. The character, too, was something like that.

However much the rest of us believed in her, she was the last in line at that fountain of certainty. Underneath the brilliant mind and the larky laugh was an agonizing shyness that kept her away from large gatherings and fueled the fondness for bourbon she had for many years. It was part of what made her reach toward Caroline and me, I think; she befriended us both when we were raising young dogs, and she saw in us a younger reflection of herself—canine-infatuated introverts—that made us part of a string of surrogate daughters she raised over the years.

She was an unrepentant atheist, a political progressive. She also managed, without contradiction, to be a real estate tycoon and savvy investor, all on a teacher's salary and with a poker face and a great deal of nerve. That economics degree, tucked away like the pedigree, was never mentioned but never absent. She dressed in old sweaters and jeans and probably looked in a mirror only to check her teeth for spinach. Her tree house of an apartment in Cambridge—easily affordable after she had bought and flipped, bought and flipped—was filled with antiques, most of which she had found, and with geraniums that bloomed year-round. The kitchen was a large room with six windows she had never bothered to renovate, furnished with old file cabinets and a Depression era–sized refrigerator. There was a floral couch in the corner, and I used to pile on the couch with the dogs and a mug of tea and everything in me would relax.

She taught me about houses and the stock market and perennials and training a dog off-lead, and what things she didn't know were mostly a result of her age. She was as bad on the computer as she was good with investments, so when the world was first going online, she asked me to help her set up her stock portfolio (buried in many lucrative cubbies across investment houses) so that she could track it online in real time. I phoned the morning of our date and told her to get all her statements together and I'd be over.

When I arrived she had coffee ready and a pile of papers in a file by the computer, and I sat down and found the site I wanted, ready to start transferring data. Marjorie put a hand on my wrist to stop me.

"I have a confession to make," she said, and when I looked up she was grinning. "I'm loaded!"

I laughed. "Why am I not surprised?" I said, and then she opened the files to her precious statements, various caches of blue chips and bonds and complex investments that she had bought and held and held and held.

Ah, years since she's gone, and she gives me such pleasure still.

We talked for hours over the years about deeper things: how to die and being alone and the great hurdles and benefits of having, both of us, stayed single. The last year that Caroline was alive, a few months before she got sick, she and Marjorie took me to dinner on my birthday, a cold night in January when it was difficult to feel much cheer. It was 2002; I was fifty-one, and had bought my first house in Marjorie's neighborhood six months earlier. She and I said good night to Caroline at the restaurant and drove home together. Sitting outside my house in the warm car and the cold dark, Marjorie turned to me and said, apropos of nothing, "I don't think having a husband would have changed your life. But I do think having a house will." It was pure Marjorie, a quirky and precise birthday blessing, and more than a decade later, I believe she was right.

She had a coterie of friends, men and women, gay and straight, parents and teachers and dog lovers and rebels of various kinds, and though she could barely tolerate seeing more than a few of us at a time, we lined up to love her. Listened to her rail about the bond market or the crime of no universal healthcare.

On the phone with Marjorie, when you mentioned a date coming up or asked a question and she had to put the phone down, she had one response: "Hold the wire!" she would say briskly, an anachronism from yesteryear, and I felt a little glee every time she said it. Caroline and I once confessed to each other that we both baited her, invented reasons to get her to say, "Hold the wire!" She took notes on everything, even our commonplace, feeble advice. It was the rest of us who should have been listening to her.

I knew Marjorie for just less than twenty years, during which time I got dogs, got Caroline, had a lot of everything I loved and had to lose most of it. And Marjorie was unafraid of it all. She never flinched in the face of grief, never once diminished its reach or treated it other than the grand mystery it was. She had lost her mother when she was relatively young, and a sister when she was in her fifties, and she knew about losing what you couldn't stand to lose. On this battlefield she was a warrior, and I can see her now: Striding into my backyard the morning of Caroline's death, the first to dare to find me, her arms outreached and a huge smile on her face. Saying to me, weeks later, when I broke down on her front porch without warning, "It will come over you like a thunderstorm, and sometimes go just as quickly." Counseling me to forgive the friends who fled pain or said the wrong thing or couldn't help; she knew I had bigger things to tend than resentment. She stayed close while I buried my best friend, both parents, and a beloved dog, and somehow she taught me about staying the course. About accepting death not as an enemy, but as a natural end of the story—an outcome, insouciant and certain, like rain or night.

Marjorie's biggest regret was not having had children, and this made me sad because she viewed it as her wrongdoing, a personal failing instead of the dice roll that life can be. The truth is that she nurtured so carefully and widely—her students, her border collies, her friends—that I can't help thinking we'd have all missed out a little if she'd had her own kids.

In that sense she did have children, and the closest of them was Betsy, a former student and then teacher, former tenant and then housemate, finally, thoroughly, the friend and surrogate daughter Marjorie counted on. When Betsy married and had children, Marjorie rented the downstairs of her two-family house in Cambridge to the four of them, then converted the property into condominiums so they could all stay together.

I have a picture taken the summer of 2008, the day after I had flown home with Tula when she was a nine-week-old Samoyed puppy. I had lost Clementine, my first Sam, a few months earlier, and now here was Marjorie, there for birth and death alike, marching into the backyard to meet the youngest member of our tribe. In the photo an aged Cory is sitting nearby, looking peaceable but alarmed at the competition, and Marjorie is sitting with her knees folded under her—past seventy, the old field hockey player with the straight back and legs of steel. She's holding Tula, all eleven pounds of her, and appraising her with the cool eye of a woman who has known dogs for a half century. I remember her turning to me that day just after the photo was taken, just after she had put Tula on the grass and we were both watching her explore her new world. "Do you love her yet?" she asked me, knowing that the notion of instant love wasn't guaranteed, but also that, if I didn't yet, I would.

She lost Cory two years later, and I took her a bouquet with a tennis ball buried in the middle, and we both cried. Because I couldn't imagine her without a border collie, I offered to co-raise a puppy with her, a foolish idea but testament to what they meant to her and she meant to me. By then she had moved part-time to a Quaker retirement community in New Hampshire, and she had taken Cory with her for his last couple of years. Every dog she had was the one she loved most, and you got the sense that she was taking all of them with her into the great beyond.

A place that she adamantly did not believe in. That's me being sentimental again, imagining Cory and Marjorie in the next meadow, and I feel sure she would laugh and allow me that fantasy, enjoying it herself but not embracing it. She lived another three years, and the body that had been so strong began to fail her in alarming ways. Her last summer in Cambridge, she told me matter-of-factly that she wouldn't last a year.

She also asked, without a trace of drama, if I would help her figure out a way to die in the event of suffering. I don't know that she asked anyone else, but I'd be surprised if she didn't: Marjorie could be almost laughably pragmatic. She was trying to assign the right job to the right person, and she knew I was a diligent researcher and would not quake before the request.

I placated her, fended her off. I knew she loved her physician in New Hampshire and told her to have a frank conversation with her, and then I went about doing my little online research, finding out what I already knew: It would not be easy, or simple, to check out swiftly, without the right medical team and laws to protect you. I half-prayed for death to come on its little cat feet and take her. With the same efficiency as the exquisite perennials in her garden, she had become frail almost overnight. What one hoped for now was a hard freeze.

Indeed, she died in deep winter, during a bitter February in New Hampshire, where she had returned at the end of autumn. A constellation of conditions had caused an aspiration pneumonia that showed no sign of abating, and she handled this medical reality with a forthrightness that caught us all off guard but surprised no one. When Betsy got to New Hampshire, a few hours after her doctors had told her she wouldn't get better, Marjorie simply announced, "There's been a change of plan"—as though she were in charge of even this last task. She refused fluids and any kind of intervention, understanding that she would slip into unconsciousness within a matter of hours. Then she settled into her recliner with a photograph of Cory and with Betsy by her side. When Betsy asked if she wanted her to call anyone, Marjorie was firm on that, too. "No," she told her. "I trust my relationships." And then she added something else: "Tell everyone I wasn't afraid." Within the hour, she closed her eyes and died.

It was a no-nonsense gift flung to us all, a last wave before she left the field. At the service at Shady Hill two months later, there was a large overhead screen showing projected images of young Marjorie, gorgeous Marjorie, the girl on a pony, the woman with her head thrown back laughing. She was stunning; she filled up the screen with what looked to be a brimming life. But the image I hold close when I think of her is from a day in her midseventies, one summer afternoon in Cambridge. We were on opposite sides of the little main street in our neighborhood, and she hadn't seen me yet, so I had caught her in a state of unaware grace. She was wearing an old Arizona State University T-shirt (a place I doubt she had ever been), baggy shorts, a fisherman's hat, and a pair of throwaway optometrist's sunglasses—the plastic ones they give you after dilating your eyes. (She thought them perfectly serviceable, so always wore them until they fell apart.) Cory was at heel, gazing up at her as though she were the Queen of England, and she was smiling and talking to him as they loped along. She looked preposterously beautiful, and my heart filled when I saw her there—stripped of all encumbrances and useless vanities, as free in that moment as thistle on the wind.

18

"I t is bound to be very imperfect," Virginia Woolf wrote in her journal, when she was beginning work on the novel that would become *The Waves*. "But I think it possible that I have got my statues against the sky."

The image is pure Woolf, majestic and lonely even in a diary entry, and it captures something exact about the writer's experience. I printed out the quote and taped it on the wall of my upstairs study, next to a pen drawing I did of Tula sleeping, next to the Post-it notes with writing ideas, next to the telegram from my dad to my mother at the end of the Second World War.

And yet lately the image has seemed sad. A frozen garden of perfection, impermeable only so long as no one moves.

I created this room, this second-floor aerie, as a

place where I could be off the grid, even from myself. My country house, I called it, when I bought the upstairs apartment of a two-family home and doubled my living space. I made a rule that here I wrote in longhand only. No cellphones, keyboards. Only a stack of clutter, a jar of pens and pencils, a few empty legal pads, far less majestic than Woolf's statues but just as silently waiting.

Now that you have your room, Woolf asks in her famous "Professions for Women," "How are you going to furnish it . . . ? With whom are you going to share it, and upon what terms?" I've not had to worry about this last question; the only people who come up here uninvited are my neighbor Peter and Tyler, and both are happy to be escorted downstairs as soon as I rise. As Tyler says, "Nothing's ever *happening* up here." When Peter comes up he is with his Belgian, Shiloh, usually rowdy and whistling for me and for Tula, and yet his voice always softens by the time they get to the top of the stairs. It's not me; it's the room. Like it's absorbed years and years of quiet, and elicits the same.

What is in the room matters greatly to me, even though I placed everything here quickly and without much forethought. An old poster of a perilously long sentence from Proust, diagrammed, on the mantel over the black fireplace. Several photos in a line: Caroline rowing on a lake in New Hampshire; our two dogs looking out the window that same summer. An action shot of Clementine, lure coursing in Vermont. Another picture of Tula in my lap when she was a year old—she was in full winter coat, and the angle of the photo makes it look as though I am holding a lion. And a close-up of a muscled arm: Caroline's bicep, a photo she thought was funny but that I so loved she gave it to me.

Also: The saltcellar from the kitchen table at the farmhouse in east Texas where my dad grew up. A long piece of sweetgrass a friend gave me to bless the house. A rickety drafting table that Peter and I found on the street a decade ago, now covered with half drafts and books and notes to myself. Propped in the corner is a gingham doll that a novelist friend decorated for me when I moved my study up here. She is my totem, a geeky companion. She has a pencil strapped across her chest, weaponized, and Louise reminded me when she sent it that the doll was my muse. (In return I sent her a crimson red puppet with flowing silver hair.) And over the fireplace, blue lights. In the past year, a Buddhist prayer flag across the windows. But I'll get to that soon enough.

I flung the inkpot a long time ago, to go back to Woolf. Used it as a weapon on that iconic angel in the house, the one with the male-bestowed sainthood who feasted on the bones of the female creative spirit. She died hard, Woolf wrote, inspiring a century of women since. So: No demanding angels here, asking for dinner or self-sacrifice or fine etiquette. Just me. Me and the dog and a clock with no hands, a schedule based on when my body gets hungry or needs a walk. A spartan bargain, one with a few great moments and a multitude of stillness, some of it brutal. These days when I climb the stairs my mind starts to bend a little, unfold, toward some familiar clearing in the woods. Sometimes it's scary; I can't always take it. Some days I just sit in the chair and look out the window. Every so often, on winter afternoons, I dance.

TYLER'S BIRTHDAY LIST,
dictated by Tyler to Gail at age five,
on occasion of sixth birthday
(several months away)

white standard poodle female or male
porcupine hat with REAL quills!
a ferret named Winky
a banana
a parrot named Polly who says *That's annoying!*
a chocolate cookie house
flute or recorder
saber-tooth tiger tooth if it's appropriate
(substitute: Tula's baby tooth)
possibility: generic necklace

BIRTHDAY LIST, TWO YEARS LATER

"What do you want for your birthday this year?" I ask.

She seems uninterested in the question; she is

separating the chocolate chips from a cookie, to save them for last. Finally, a benign shrug. "Nothing."

"Nothing!" I say. "You always want things! We usually make a list."

"OK," she says. "You as a best friend."

I pause just a split, and say, "Well, that's easy. Is that all?"

She shrugs again. "I'm growing up."

19

The first frost in Cambridge came late this year, and while I always have to scramble to haul in the garden's survivors, it's usually clear what goes and what stays. Dahlias get dug up and stored in the basement. Tuberous begonias and geraniums are cut back and moved to the sunporch. I strip the hibiscus, leaf by leaf, the way my friend Rocco taught me, and let them go semi-dormant until spring. My high-maintenance ferns I pamper, swear at, and inevitably give prime location, where they shed and annoy me all winter. The other flowering annuals are thrown out, their pots stored upside down before the freeze.

This year, though, I couldn't give it up. I meant to be ruthless, but things changed after dark. I repotted coleus on the back porch, where it was 38 degrees, even though the plants were already leggy and dropping leaves. I scooped up a calibrachoa and took it into the kitchen, where it lost half its vine as soon as I got it inside. I made bouquets out of the trimmings and created a fern hospital for the five scraggly ones I couldn't toss. I hung on to pitiful plants I couldn't even name, and there was no room now for the scarlet-red cyclamen that usually hauled my heart through winter. I would make room, tomorrow. But tonight the low living room lights made everything look so green and alive and not yet cold, framed by the dark outside.

I did all this because the thing I most wanted to save I could not, and she lay dozing on the back porch while I came and went. Tula had turned nine in summer with quiet fanfare, which is to say I had cooked her a little hamburger and put a candle in it, and we had lived through another day. She had been diagnosed in January with inoperable liver cancer and given a matter of weeks to live—weeks, I had been warned, in which I would have to be vigilant, in the event she collapsed from an internal bleed. I slept with my phone in hand, carried driving directions to two veterinary hospitals in my wallet, and calculated on every short walk how far I could go before I was out of range of help. By June she had outlived two prognoses; by autumn, a good friend was calling her Lazarus. But I knew. She had dropped a few times, always at home, sagged when her blood pressure plummeted and then leaned up against me, taken a two-hour nap.

She was in no pain, this I knew and had been assured. She was in fact living the life of Riley, eating noodles with chicken gravy and being fussed over by every kid on the block. She was not looking at her baby pictures, like I was, or weeping in the next room, or messing around with spent plants in the freezing dark. She was a born Buddhist and knew how to let go. Me, not so much.

"Deciduous" is from the Latin *decidere*, to fall down, also ephemeral or not lasting. "Perennial," also from Latin, meaning to last the year through, as well as abiding, enduring, unending, unfailing, undying. A resurrection from the earth each spring, different for flora and fauna. We attach ourselves to lion cubs but are happy to settle for the rebirth of yarrow or peonies, flowers merely related to their origin, not the thing itself. Yet another argument for the charity of impermanence.

And "annual," from the Latin for year, and "mortal," the origin of which is death. Only one of these words is not about time, but rather about the end of it, or the eclipse of it. The dog will die and I will love her perennially, until I fall, too.

I got the green thumb from both sides of the family, though being able to grow things in Texas was a given, especially if you came from farming families. There is a picture of a wee me in my father's lap sitting in his backyard garden, sometime in the 1950s, and the corn and tomatoes are so high I look like a foundling. He could make anything bear fruit and taste good enough to spoil you for life. My mother's gift was color, a hallucinatory magic. Her pansies bloomed at Christmas and looked as though she'd fed them psilocybin. As she aged and grew slightly addled about her gardening skills, she swore the only treatment she gave her four-foot jade plant was to whack it with a broom once a month. No water, she said. I didn't believe her, but her ninety-year-old irrationality about what worked was still admirable in its conviction.

By mid-autumn I was steeling myself for saying goodbye to what seemed like everything at once. Peter and Pat, whose dog Shiloh had grown up with Tula, were moving to Northern California. We had co-raised two generations of dogs together, and for fifteen years wandered in and out of one another's nearby houses as though life were one big college dorm. And Shiloh, now twelve, had just been diagnosed with heart failure. They were hoping to get her to her new home before she died.

Pat and I spent the end of the summer walking the neighborhood at night. "You can't leave now," I said, preposterously, sounding like Tyler when she hollered *NOOOOO* about something she didn't like. "If you leave now I can't take it. It will be a quadruple assault." Our two wolflike dogs walked ahead of us in step, content and beautiful, ebony and ivory, into the waning light of late August. One evening Pat found a baby rabbit in the street, far from any greenery or possible nest. In an instant she had scooped it up and placed it in the crook of her elbow, and then carried it the mile back to our houses. She made it a box, put it in the hedges of the park next door, fussed over it, moved it, revisited it, worried. There were probably hundreds of newborn rabbits that week within a half-mile radius, but this one, this tar-and-concrete renegade, had our attention. If fretting and caretaking guaranteed an auspicious future, that rabbit could have gotten into Harvard. She couldn't let it go.

That was pretty much how I felt about their leaving.

They left in late October, and Shiloh slept on my couch until they were ready to drive away. She got as far as the front porch, leaning up against me after the humans had hugged goodbye, and Peter finally had to pick her up and carry her to the waiting car. What her reluctance meant I can't know: Maybe she was just sleepy, maybe she didn't want to split up the pack by leaving me and Tula. But it was an *Old Yeller* moment that became the image, for me, of what it meant to lose them all.

For the next couple of months it was just the two of us. I spent weeks cleaning up the fall garden, fussing over meadow rue and sweet peas so that I might be surrounded, day after day, by dust unto dust. I stayed out there till dusk, until my hands cracked from the dirt, and I became wildly happy when I saw a late-season bumper crop of wildflowers. I needed to be reminded, all the time, of the perennial fact of life, of Willa Cather's exquisite description of lying in the pumpkin patch and floating into the perfect stillness, in *My Ántonia*—"when we die and become a part of something entire." It was a balm on my tired heart. Tula lay nearby in the pachysandra while I worked, and I wanted to lie down next to her and let the weeds and nasturtiums fold over us and obliterate our sorrow.

Tyler, with the wonderful egocentrism of a seven-year-old, believes she has much to teach Tula before she's gone. I hope she lives a month, she tells me, so that I can advance her to the next level of genie training. I ask Tyler if she can fix me while she's at it—fix a broken heart. No, she tells me, that requires a heart genie, and it's special training I don't have.

I think she's fudging, and tell her so. Since when has she balked at any genie challenge? I thought you could fix anything, I say. You said I could come to you in dark of night and you would know what to do.

She sighs, as though the responsibility of being seven and in charge of my heart is just too much, but more like she's irritated and busy, rather than over- whelmed. "Well, I can call up the heart genies," she tells me. "But it may take them a while to get here." It is the first time I've laughed in weeks.

When Tula was first diagnosed I checked her breath every time I could, meaning that I awoke about thirty times a night to hear the music of that one breath, remembering what it was like not to hear it, nine years ago when my first dog died. I swore then that I would never love another dog like Clementine, because I loved her so much that I could not bear her leaving. Then I fell in love with her monster replacement, a gorgeous eleven-pound puppy who grew into a fifty-five-pound adult and who turned into the world's best dog. They all become the world's best dog, even the worst dog, when you love them.

She is an animal who has spent her entire life with me. I am an animal who has spent only a small part of my life with her, though now, this long minute, it seems like forever and not nearly long enough.

This is what love usually means, unless you both go down without a blip of warning.

I sit somewhere near her and have the same vocabulary. I'm over here. Lie down on your bed. Good girl. Pond. Park. Noodles.

I give her rigatoni for dinner, right out of the pan. I season the noodles with chicken gravy and Parmesan cheese, cool the pan with cold water and let her have the whole damn thing on the floor. She looks up at me as though she has won the lottery. She is having a great life up until the end, partly because she doesn't know it's the end, has no fear, no pain. She lives only in the present and enjoys every noodle.

Anticipatory grief is the clinical term for what I'm going through, a suspended state of waiting for the anguish that must lie ahead. The curse of consciousness: an ability to contemplate pain yet unknown. Walking today at the cemetery, the first early snow of late autumn, I tear up at Tula's pure wolflike joy, running like a young dog. When she sleeps after we get home I sing songs to her on the back porch, made-up songs about Clementine, and Caroline, the blond woman in heaven with many dogs in her lap. This is probably ridiculous, but my voice soothes Tula and the stories appease me. The promise of an afterlife, real or not, pulled out like the old tattered velveteen rabbit whenever we need it.

I often wonder, as I suppose everyone wonders, how I wound up here. Wouldn't have seen it, though it did occur to me recently that when I was Tyler's age I announced I was going to be a dog breeder when I grew up. I also claimed, in the next several years, that I would be a mathematician, a barrel racer, a writer. Never a wife, oddly. Not on my fantasy list. I don't know what that means, or if it means anything at all.

At the end Tula gets her days and nights mixed up. We go out for late-night walks, eleven P.M., up and down brick-lined streets in the cold, with me trying to get her as tired and calm as possible. She is anxious when we get home, when I give her room to roam, so we sleep together leashed, like we are tied to the mast on the *Titanic*.

She dies on the shortest day of the year.

Through sleep I hear a crash and don't respond. I am in the middle of a dream I don't want to leave. In the dream I opened a door to an outside breezeway, and though it was winter there were flowers everywhere—fuchsia, otherworldly plants against a snowy landscape, and a magical tree with streaming iridescent white blossoms that made me gasp. I wondered how anyone could live without this beauty. And Tula was there, a version of Tula, smaller and far away and running against the horizon.

I hear the crashing noise again and rouse myself from sleep. When I get to her she is standing a room away with one leg straight out, confused and still, and I get her back into the bedroom and onto her bed. Her gums are the color of linen. Once she is lying down, I trickle water into her mouth so that she won't be thirsty. I make a pallet next to her and lean up against the wall, the phone next to me so I can reach our vet, who loves Tula and has been waiting for this call. When I hold on to Tula's front paws with one hand, something I have done since she was a puppy, her breathing slows and so does mine.

We stay like this for a long time.

At the end of that night I hang blue lights in the upstairs windows and a Buddhist prayer flag. This is my wave at the holidays: blue shooting stars for the dead.

20

Two months later, I go to California.

As soon as I walk into the air terminal I hear Peter's unmistakable sonorous voice, laughing with some stranger at a coffee kiosk. And so I start to laugh, and then nearly cry. Maybe home is wherever somebody you love can make you laugh for no good reason from halfway across a room.

I have come to see Pat and Peter, but also Shiloh, who is mostly sleeping and on her way out. When I get out of the car at the house I whistle for her, our private whistle, and she appears at my side immediately, a silent sentinel. She lies next to my bed all night. I feel the connection thrown wide, as though all the love I shared for years with these two magnificent creatures, Tula and Shiloh, has reached like a boomerang across the skies, Cambridge to California, death to life, and we are all OK and the love doesn't die, just its corporeal object. This is a consolation I have known before but always forget, like innocence being continually reborn.

When I lived in San Francisco I was in my early twenties, lost and poised, soaring one day and falling the next, and California appealed to all that was best and worst about that era of confusion. I worked as a paralegal in a radical women's law firm, believed I was saving the world, took drugs in Mendocino, and felt the great cloud of the future carry me into a never-never land of stoner paradise. I roll my eyes when I remember this now, because I was so joyous and melancholy at once, so free of anything that mattered, and when I left there it was by hitchhiking away from Telegraph Avenue in Berkeley. Decades later, I gave a reading in Marin County, and I told the audience that I had loved Northern California but never learned how to be a grown-up there. The audience didn't really laugh, either because (a) no one knows how to be a grown-up in California or (b) they thought I was insulting their home, when in fact I was speaking to the collision of California mellow with my own youthful idiocy.

I still wonder sometimes which coast would've been a better choice. If I'd stayed in California I might have been a sheep farmer or an astrologer, drunk and unhappy, in Ukiah or Mendocino. Instead I wound up a freelance writer, drunk and unhappy, in an attic garret in a cheap neighborhood in Boston. Who then walked downstairs and found my way through snowstorms and fear to the rooms where I got sober. Same hurdles, different circumstances.

I've told Peter and Pat I want to see the redwoods, so we drive to Muir Woods, a place I remember as a portal to heaven, and yet now there are neon signs miles in advance telling us we need to call ahead for parking reservations. Peter drops us off, and Pat and I walk into a timeless sanctuary of those gentle, towering beings that are the redwoods. I could lie down here and stay. Places take you to other places, and this day reminds me of one in Colorado, when I was ten or eleven, when I saw aspen trees in autumn for the first time, and realized that forests were a chapel for the heart. I feel that way today, too, and then we all drive to the beach and Shiloh and I wade into the cold Pacific.

Could I live in California? Everything feels bountiful, reachable, open here, and I know I am partly responding to the closed cavern back home where my heart has been the past few months. Here I walk miles in sunshine, swim laps in an outside pool, look at the stars. On a long woods walk with Sasha, one of Peter and Pat's daughters, we are suddenly within a few yards of a horse stable, and we crawl through the split-rail fence to talk to the horses. The woman tending them was once a rodeo princess in east Texas, she tells me, and we nuzzle the horses and I ache with happiness. In the first three stalls are splendid animals who are gradations of white: a speckled white and gray, maybe an Appaloosa, then an uppity ivory mare with a braided mane, and at the end of the row, a proud, cloud-white horse who tosses her head but then relaxes. The trio seems magical, profound, when in fact it is just the luck of the draw, the end of a beautiful day, a moment I will share with Sasha. But this evening it says something to me about that boomerang of love again, white animals giving me everything I need, and it cinches my plans for the future.

The day before I leave I lie in the grass outside with Shiloh, my head on her neck, and I sing to her and tell her goodbye. Peter tells me she keeps looking for me after I leave. Two days after I get home I will realize I have poison oak on my neck and face where I lay in the grass, probably spread by my tears when I said goodbye to her. Totally worth it.

At the airport a young woman is walking around with a large therapy pig on a leash. The pig is wearing a THERAPY PIG PET ME sign and glittery angel wings, and she has brightly painted red toenails. She is indeed charming her audiences and making everyone happy. I go to my gate, where another young woman is doing yoga headstands against the wall. She is both oblivious and smug—everything I love and don't love about California. I send Peter a photo of the pig and thank him for sending her to me. He writes back: *Take good care of the sow!*

Something happened to me in California. Something pried open the door of my closed system. I can sit in a chair in the dark and not feel alone, or fragmented— just sad, even comforted by sadness. Whole. Experience is what you get sometimes instead of joy.

Grief is like a wrestling match in the dark. It takes the wind out of you; you're exhausted, you lose your footing, it doesn't mean anything beyond its own huge self. Also you must learn it anew every time; you don't get points or skip ahead for having suffered. I cried so much the first weeks after Tula died that I was dehydrated and my eyes hurt, and the only place I couldn't cry was in the pool, at night. One evening after hours of circling doubt and despair, when I'd been turning my misery into self-blame, I went to the pool because I didn't know what else to do. And swimming I just thought, like a little kid, "I miss my girl," and then my heart broke open all over again and I was actually all right.

Tyler made me a card that I still keep on a shelf. She worried that she had misspelled words (she hadn't). It is a drawing of a giant bear-head that is Tula, surrounded by hearts and notes of encouragement:

Dear Gail,

I'm so sorry about Tula. ♥♥♥♥♥♥ But we can write a book about your dog! ♥♥

P. S. I hope you know she was ready.

Inside Tula's chest she has drawn a box with a heart in it and a girl (me) and a sign pointing to me with the name "Gail." In other words, she tells me, I am inside Tula's heart and she is inside mine. No guru or grief counselor could have been much wiser. I kiss the card, I kiss Tyler on top of her head and tell her the card is perfect, and so is she.

The thing about the endless winters in the Northeast is that you get the light back before anything else. You can be in the middle of a raging blizzard, still have seven weeks of cold and howling winds to endure, but some reckoning that makes life bearable has blessed you with the returning light, wide vision illuminated against white snow. So that even if you are hurting and desolate there is that bright panorama, that longer day, that promise.

I've learned that you must love what is in front of you, rather than only what is behind, or you will go mad from sorrow on the journey. Inhabit some careful land between the cloak of the past and what you have left ahead, even if it's just the path itself. I spend a lot of winter days walking the streets of Cambridge, go sometimes to the cemetery and past the graves where for years I've left stones. One is an ornate slab of slate eulogizing Benjamin and Sarah Peirce, who died in the late 1880s, and at the bottom of the gravestone is an epitaph, THEY HAVE OUTSOARED THE SHADOW OF OUR NIGHT. What first drew me to the grave was the mark carved at its crest: the mathematical symbol ø, for void, for null or empty set. And beneath it the inscription: THERE IS ONE GOD AND SCIENCE IS THE KNOWLEDGE OF HIM.

I was intrigued by the whole package, so I went home and researched Peirce, and learned that he was an esteemed mathematician at Harvard. A man who found a way to reconcile the beauty of pi and the golden ratio with his idea of celestial perfection. The grave seemed to me like a clue to the inside of someone's heart, a sanctum come upon by a stranger more than a century later. Peirce's son was the famous philosopher C. S. Peirce, whom I studied in school a million years ago, and now here I was at that man's father's grave, leaving behind a little rock because I had liked his ø. A void, if you will, filled merely by the act of my having seen it.

You have to drink from the fountain as often as you can, every day if possible. Doesn't have to be the Trevi. It can be from a brook, a glass of water. Just take what beauty or kindness is there—the air you breathe, the red-tailed hawk circling overhead at the Peirces' grave. Leave the rocks. Try not to be afraid. I love this grave and what it teaches me about death and hope and the great rope thrown out across the ages, like Tyler's imaginary rope when she was little, 250,000-plus-infinity miles long. I'm trying to outwalk my shadow right now, and every step is an act of faith. Every breath a ragged prayer.

21

I spend nights swimming in an indoor lap pool and watching the moon through the frosted-over glass windows. One evening at the end of winter, when it is 12 degrees outside, I run into Chris, my tall Chris, world traveler and physics teacher, who loved Tula and once told me I didn't need to go anywhere; I had a beautiful dog and a good place to swim. She is like that—itinerant but earthbound, eschewing most of life's norms. I hug her and say, "Guess where I'm going this week?" as the winds rage outside. She rolls her eyes. "Paris?" she asks, because it is a typical threat-promise of mine, that I will travel the wider world that I missed while hanging out with dogs. "No," I say, laughing. "Canada. I'm going to Canada to get a dog."

Her delight is physical. She half-hollers, she stamps her foot, her six-foot body dancing with happiness. Her eyes confirm everything I had hoped about this being right. I cannot manage to drag myself to Paris, but she knows that I will go anywhere for the right dog. The right dog is my Amalfi Coast.

My friend Justin is going with me—a man I've known for decades, my kid brother were I allowed to choose. He is tall and quiet and funny, the kind of friend you want for a road trip. Two days before we're scheduled to leave, ominous weather reports start rolling in. We are headed for the snowbelt, through upstate New York, and it will turn out to be a record-breaking March with four nor'easters. The notion of driving to Ontario for a dog during a snowstorm doesn't faze him. It doesn't faze me either, but I am no judge of sanity; I have lost my mind over the object of this trip. She is a two-year-old Samoyed, a retired show dog who just weaned her only litter of pups. The breeder picked her for me and so must have the gods, because her name (thank you, Dolly Parton) is Jolene.

The only people on the roads in the desolate country of upstate New York at this time of year are either crazy or intrepid. The intrepid one in our car is driving, while I look out the window at the stark, barren hills covered with deer, who must be foraging as the days grow longer.

Flocks of snow geese are cruising overhead, punctuating the monothematic gray of a late-winter sky. We are far outnumbered up here, species-wise, just a few humans trundling on the highway ahead of a blizzard, pointing north past a one-word road sign with an arrow: CANADA. Heading in the right direction.

Lake Ontario is a rugged sea of rime ice and waves. We stay over in a little town on its edge, so that we can head back tomorrow with the dog and maybe beat the worst of the storm. Justin is a lifelong New Englander and a good driver. I have called ahead to make a reservation; the Hilton, when we get there, is nearly empty.

On our long drive up—tomorrow's will be twice as long—I think about the different ways friends have counseled me, well-meant advice after I lost Tula. "I worry that you are trying to replace the joy of the past," a friend said, which of course is exactly what I was doing, what we all do. What he really meant was, I worry that you are too old, too slight, to handle another sled dog. Bring it on, I said, life is short. I'm going to be one of those crazy old ladies with a team of dogs, maybe Tyler's palomino; hell, I would have a dragon if I could.

But this is no dragon. She is a ghost orchid—a white doe of a Samoyed who places her paws gently on my chest when I meet her the next morning. She will turn out to be a shy dog, reserved with new people, but today she seems to know that she is mine, because she jumps in the back of my car without a hint of hesitation. I have put an old T-shirt in the crate with her and she lies down against it, and for the next ten-plus hair-raising hours that it takes us to get to Cambridge, she is completely silent. A queenly white dog looking out at a blizzard, all the way home.

Peter, three thousand miles away in California, is our self-appointed wingman. He texts every half hour, telling me what the weather reports say, even though we are driving through near whiteout conditions and could be a meteorologist's storm trackers. *Stay on Mass Pike all the way,* he writes, as though there is anywhere else to go. I am cheered by his California navigation, interrupted only by phone calls from two other men friends who can't believe we dared to make this trip. When I reply to my friend Jim with a photo of Jolene, surrounded by our world of white, he texts me back, *Gail, that's a dog you have there.* From him, the highest of praise.

We drive up to my house at ten-thirty P.M. We have crawled home, past spinouts and deserted rest stops, at 35 mph. My old Subaru got us here but so did the men in my life, one driving, one spotting us long-distance, several checking in along the way. The brothers I always wanted and now am blessed with. Jolene will be reserved around strangers, but she will love Justin from that day on, and has an affinity for big, soft-spoken men. She has good instincts, and so do I.

Some days I fear that I have cheated grief, haven't suffered enough, because Jolene reminds me of everything I loved about both Clementine and Tula, but this makes me happy, not sad, and the lonely purposeless fog that had enveloped me is gone. And then my friend Andrea, poet and realist, laughs at my worry and tells me I have suffered plenty. Tells me that being a shepherd is a calling, one with my name on it, and Jolene is my newest charge.

Tyler's visits are shorter and less frequent these days—she is on her way to the park to shoot hoops, or is hanging with friends, or has after-school track or riding. I know this is as it should be. She is like a star that fell from the sky into my yard. I have done my job of becoming a good memory in the making. She is eight going on thirty, thinks she will be at least six two as an adult, and plans to start a national polo team. When I say one day, torn between humor and self-pity, that she will forget me, she says, "Don't be ridiculous."

One afternoon she is grumpy, or stormy, as she would say, and announces that she has decided to banish almost everyone from the world, with the exception of her family and the new utopia she has created and will lead. She names who she will keep: her cousins, most of her class at school, the track team. At the end of the long list she adds me, along with a teacher she likes. I am glad but surprised. You mean you'll have adults in the new world? I ask. She shrugs. "I need *some* guidance."

The first time I saw the Peirce grave with the ø, the empty set symbol, I mistook it for infinity, which is ∞. I fostered this misread for months, though I should have known better: I used to be a math whiz. So my error must have been a matter of want, the unconscious see-ing *forever* instead of *nothing.* Horizons, not emptiness. I grew up where the horizon was an icon of each, some-thing endless but not necessarily bountiful, and so maybe ø and ∞, to me and in the world, can seem like the same thing.

I think you need to be able to handle both. You need to know that genies will grow up and disappear, that dogs and friends and loved ones will leave you, that everything in life, including life itself, depends upon the transience of others as well as the kindness. You have to let forever blur into that one line of memory out there. You have to walk toward the mirage.

ACKNOWLEDGMENTS

Early flashes of this story emerged through a series of rich conversations with Louise Erdrich, and my gratitude to her is on every page. My editor, Kate Medina, and my agent, Lane Zachary, were central in their support and acuity; thanks to them both for believing in me and in the need for this book. The folks at Random House have been great caretakers over the years. Thank you, Avideh Bashirrad, for being my star catcher this time around.

Andrea Cohen provided the unrivaled listening skills of a poet and good friend. I'm also grateful to Peter and Pat Wright, Judy Weinstock, Tink Davis, and Jean Kilbourne. Dick Chasin offered wisdom and essential humor. Finally, my thanks to Shannon Davies, Nancy Hays, Eliza Gagnon, and the Soeur Queens, for reminding me how powerful sisterhood really is.

ABOUT THE AUTHOR

GAIL CALDWELL is the author of three previous memoirs, including the bestselling *Let's Take the Long Way Home*. She was the chief book critic of *The Boston Globe* for more than twenty years, and in 2001 received the Pulitzer Prize for distinguished criticism. She lives in Cambridge, Massachusetts.

ABOUT THE TYPE

This book was set in Baskerville, a typeface designed by John Baskerville (1706–75), an amateur printer and typefounder, and cut for him by John Handy in 1750. The type became popular again when the Lanston Monotype Corporation of London revived the classic roman face in 1923. The Mergenthaler Linotype Company in England and the United States cut a version of Baskerville in 1931, making it one of the most widely used typefaces today.